Business forecasting
and planning

Business forecasting and planning

PETER SHEARER

PRENTICE HALL

New York London Toronto Sydney Tokyo Singapore

First published 1994 by
Prentice Hall International (UK) Limited
Campus 400, Maylands Avenue
Hemel Hempstead
Hertfordshire, HP2 7EZ
A division of
Simon & Schuster International Group

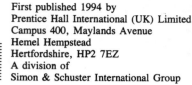

Typeset in 10/12pt Times
by MHL Typesetting Ltd, Coventry

Printed and bound in Great Britain by
Redwood Books , Trowbridge, Wiltshire

Library of Congress Cataloging-in-Publication Data

A catalogue record for this book is available from the Library
of Congress

ISBN 0-13-094962-0 (pbk)

British Library Cataloguing in Publication Data

A catalogue record for this book is available from
the British Library

ISBN 0-13-094962-0 (pbk)

1 2 3 4 5   98 97 96 95 94

Contents

Introduction   *vii*

1. Why forecast?   1
2. Exploratory data analysis   9
3. Residual analysis   22
4. Dirty data   35
5. Short-term forecasting 1: One-step-ahead forecasts   40
6. Short-term forecasting 2: Autoregressive models   52
7. Medium-term forecasting 1: The trade cycle   63
8. Medium-term forecasting 2: Forecasting cyclical series   76
9. Medium-term forecasting 3: Trend-curve analysis   84
10. Long-term forecasting 1: The construction cycle   94
11. Long-term forecasting 2: The long wave   103
12. Long-term forecasting 3: Delphi, scenarios and shocks   111
13. Long-term forecasting 4: Regression assumptions   119
14. Long-term forecasting 5: Regression topics   125
15. Long-term forecasting 6: Correlation analysis   132
16. New product models   141
17. Price and margin forecasting   154
18. A company planning model   160
19. Monitoring   165
20. Seasonal adjustment   171

Appendix   Durbin—Watson test   179
References   180
Further reading   181
Index   182

Introduction

Forecasting is a much-maligned activity. Forecaster-bashing is an easy occupation because forecasts are almost always wrong, at least to some degree. And yet forecasting continues to play a prominent role in business life — for example, Thomas and DaCosta (1979) showed that 88 per cent of large companies used forecasting in their management science studies. The reason is not hard to discover. All businesses are concerned with strategy for the future. In order to plan for a better future it is clearly necessary to anticipate the economic climate in which that strategy has to be worked out. In addition, we need to forecast our own sales, margins and so on using the economic projections. It is no use claiming that the future cannot be foretold — that just means there is no reason for making strategic decisions such as increasing advertising. We need to be fairly sure that the increased market share and profit achieved by increasing advertising are worth more than the cost of the advertising itself. Seat-of-the-pants forecasting used to be in vogue in the 1960s when not too much harm could be done by such activities — profits were easy to earn in those days. However, the decline of 'I know my market best' forecasts in favour of more structured analysis in the tougher economic environment now apparent is backed up by studies which indicate that quantitative techniques do better on average than 'expert opinion'.

This book reflects this situation, and draws on many years of business forecasting and planning in a major multinational company. The emphasis is on techniques which are in use in the business world, and the viewpoint is that which a practitioner in the business world will recognize. In particular, forecasting is not seen as an end in itself, but as an integrated part of the forecasting/planning/decision-making process. In this context interpretation for management is seen as an important element of the forecasting activity. Simple methods are preferred to complex ones — recent studies have shown that mathematically complex models often do not perform as well as older and simpler techniques. The importance of integrating the socio-economic, economic and business environments is stressed. Many texts do not differentiate between the approaches needed for short-term forecasting as distinct from medium-term or long-term methods. This is an omission which is remedied here: different sections of the book deal with forecasting and planning over the various time horizons.

Much of the material here reflects current practice in industry. We consider forecasts of 'when' an event will happen (for instance, when will the downturn end?) as well as 'what' (what level will our sales reach in five years' time?). We consider how best to forecast sales and margins in a cyclical industry. We consider the impact on various industries of the trade cycle in the economy and its impact on key business variables such as stock levels. Case studies and examples are presented, most of which have an international flavour.

Most of all, we challenge the call that nothing in the world can be forecast, and show how the needs of the business world for credible forecasts integrated with effective planning can be met.

This text should be of use both to the business practitioner and to the business school student. The book could form the basis of a final-year optional course in a first degree, and is also suitable for use in an MBA or DMS programme. Business school students will need as a prerequisite the normal first-year quantitative methods course common to most business degrees, although numerical complexity is not extensive.

The aim is not to teach the business student how to use all relevant statistical techniques. Procedures such as multiple regression, stepwise regression and ridge regression are dealt with fairly speedily in this book. If the cursory examination of these methods confuses the student then it is suggested that he/she consult a statistical text which deals with the subjects more fully; if the reader is a practitioner then the best course is to consult a professional statistician. Here we try to concentrate on the forecasting process without being side-tracked too much by the underlying statistics. We do need, however, to refer to these more difficult techniques since they are available on such well-used forecasting packages as STATGRAPHICS which can deal with most of the methods discussed in this book.

PETER SHEARER
July 1993

CHAPTER 1

Why forecast?

1.1 Introduction

We live in an ever-moving environment. Not only do we experience month-to-month variation in business activity when things are going smoothly, but we are also beset by apparently unpredictable events such as the Gulf War. Surely such environmental chaos renders any forecast useless? Indeed, the recent development of mathematical chaos theory has been misinterpreted by many as 'proof' that structured forecasts are doomed regardless of their context or purpose. And yet businesses around the world continue to treat forecasting as a high-profile activity. Thomas and Da Costa (1979) showed that forecasting was by far the most popular management science technique employed by large corporations. The UK-based Industrial Marketing Research Association (IMRA) also carried out a survey which put forecasting ahead of all other market research functions (see Chisnall 1986: 246).

So why do companies around the world set such store by forecasting? The main reason is the need to produce forecasts to underpin the planning process. Every company needs to plan for the future, whether that plan relates to the general shape of the company, or the number of widgets to order from the supplier this month. Plans concern the future and therefore invoke a need to predict the future environment as well as the future parameters of the business which will relate to that environment. Forecasting provides the bridge between the known past and the unknown future. All forecasts attempt to look below the surface chaos to find underlying patterns which should remain relevant in the future. Sometimes we may wish to investigate what will happen if deviations from these underlying patterns occur. This is known as scenario planning, and we shall meet it again in Chapter 12. However, whatever assumptions we make, there remains a need to provide forecasts to support the planning process.

A major advantage of successful forecasting is that we stand to gain competitive advantage. We *anticipate* developments, and leave the competition to *react* to events rather than to control them. The financial benefits of this can be very great. Indeed, new strategic possibilities are often opened up through the cash saved by successful forecasting.

Finally, we must be careful not to dismiss any variable as 'unforecastable'. For example, share prices have been shown to follow a 'random walk' on a daily basis. This does not imply that share prices are unpredictable. To take an obvious (but less than useful) example,

I could forecast with reasonable certainty that in 20 years' time share prices will be higher than they are now.

1.2   What do companies forecast?

There are three main levels of forecast: macro-economic data; market data; and company data. Any business is affected by general economic variables such as industrial production, the exchange rate and the price of natural raw materials such as oil. In addition, cost planning requires data on inflation rates, and human resource pressures will be influenced by unemployment. Businesses can choose whether or not to produce their own forecasts of these macro-economic variables: smaller companies will probably opt to use one of the many generally available macro-economic forecasts such as the OECD forecast or, in the UK, the Treasury forecast, the Bank of England forecast or the Henley Centre forecast. Other European countries also boast publicly available forecasts from central government sources, the central bank and so on.

A second level of forecast takes place at the level of market aggregates. We may, for example, be one of 20 PVC producers in the western European market. We are clearly interested in forecasts for the total PVC market in western Europe, perhaps also by country. Our own company's sales data are too variable from month to month to provide a reliable estimate of market growth, and in any case the movements in our market share will further cloud the picture. We need to use total market data, often collected from the various producers on a confidential basis by a trade association or other neutral body. This body will feed back to the member companies data on the total market, and such data can be used to construct a forecast.

Finally (and most importantly), we need to forecast our own business indicators. Although sales volume is very important, we should also forecast prices, margins, profits and cash. These forecasts must be consistent — there is no use providing separate forecasts for each of these indicators which fail to add up in the accounting sense. To ensure that forecasts are consistent, we often use a planning model (see Chapter 18).

1.3   Time horizons

Sometimes we need to forecast or plan for the immediate future. Sometimes we want to ensure that the long-term shape of the company is going to be right. Formalized planning procedures often fit between these two extremes and look one to three years ahead. It is useful to define time horizons as follows: short-term, up to 12 months ahead; medium-term, 1–3 years ahead; long-term, over 3 years ahead. These are not hard and fast definitions, but form a useful shorthand for many of the forecasts discussed in this book. Many forecasting techniques work better in one of these time domains than in the others. Many company departments concentrate on some of these time horizons at the expense of others. For these reasons much of the forecasting methodology discussed in this book is to be found in separate chapters on short-, medium- or long-term techniques. This will hopefully reduce the chance of the practitioner 'stretching' a short-term method for use in the long term (or vice versa).

1.4 Forecasting by department

One of the features of business forecasting is that it is pervasive: most company departments need to forecast, and they need to integrate the forecasts in a coherent manner if a sensible overall corporate strategy is to be achieved. The following are examples of forecasting interests by department in a large organization:

Marketing: Interested in both the product markets and the company's sales in those markets. Forecasts of sales volume will be made for the markets, whereas the analysis will be extended to price, gross margin and profit for company sales. Forecasts range from short-term (for tactical price-setting and volume campaign plans) to medium-term (for the company's budget review). Long-term forecasts are usually reserved for new product launches, where the board of directors will sanction new plant on the basis of long-term pay-back.

Accounts: Financial forecasts by product, consolidated into a company total forecast by the 'bottom-up' process (forecasting the products and adding up the forecasts). A wide range of financial variables will be considered — for example, turnover, profit, stocks, debtors, creditors, cash and capital expenditure. The forecasts tend to be short- and medium-term only, and often lean heavily on assumptions made by the planning department and/or the board. Often the product forecasts for operating variables are taken directly from marketing departments.

Production: An emphasis on short-term tactical variables such as throughput, stocks and grade range. Forecasting is often part of the materials requirements planning (MRP) process, and is usually heavily computerized and automated due to the frequency and sheer volume of forecasts required.

Personnel: Here the emphasis is on long-term succession planning, with the aim of providing continuity by means of a good age-range and skills distribution. The methodology is somewhat different from that employed in the commercial areas. A secondary sphere of activity is that of crisis planning: how to plan a medium-term response to the needs of a new major product, or indeed how to deal with the surplus human resources arising from the deletion of a product from the range; and how such plans affect the forecasts of age-range and skills distribution.

Management services: Again non-financial variables are forecast — for example, what computing networks, hardware and software will be needed in ten years time; how to instigate a plan to fulfil such needs.

Planning: The planning department is often a powerful board support operation, charged with providing environmental forecasts which other departments will use as a basis for their own forecasts. The planners will also be expected to combine departmental forecasts and to prepare a forecast for the company as a whole (a 'top-down' forecast) with which the aggregated departmental forecasts can be compared. The planning department will be high-profile politically as it is in a position to advise the board on the planning implications of the various forecasts being fed through it (often in conjunction with the accounts department).

Successful planning demands that *all* the forecasting inputs are recognized in any plan of action. For example, it is all too easy to concentrate on the financial implications of a course of action while assuming that manpower needs will fall into line with that course of action without difficulty. It is also very easy to look very carefully at short-term forecasts without considering long-term reactions to the short-term decisions. For example, we could react to a period of adversity by stopping recruitment for a number of years. This minimizes redundancy costs and is cost-effective in the short term. However, in the longer term the resultant gap in our age profile increases the possibility that valuable skills will be lost to retirement at much the same time. At that stage we will need to engage in the costly recruitment of workers who have already been trained by other companies, in order to rebuild a sensible age profile and skills distribution.

1.5   Integration between departments

A number of departments may be interested in the various forecasts which a company provides. For example, a short-term forecast of sales, stocks, grades and so on which emanates from an MRP package would be of interest principally to the production department, but also to sales and marketing. Because of this multiple interest in the forecast, it would tend to be produced on a regular basis. The following are examples of regular forecasts:

Weekly forecasts: Stocks, sales, grades — of interest to production, sales and marketing departments in order, for example, to plan for a sales campaign on particular product lines.

Monthly forecasts: Sales, margins, profits — of interest to marketing, accounts and planning departments. The company's monthly performance is summarized and compared with achievements in recent months and with the planned performance anticipated at the last annual review; on the basis of this the monthly forecast is updated. The aggregated forecast for the whole company would be considered at the monthly board meeting, and implications for company tactics and strategy discussed. In short, the monthly forecast is a business forecast which analyzes recent history, highlights current trends and projects these trends to provide an updated forecast.

Annual forecasts: Sales, margins, profits and cash — of interest to accounts, planning and most other departments, but largely for the board's benefit. The annual forecasts may be an integral part of the annual budget review at which a budget is set for the following year and indicative forecasts provided for another two years. Most of the company's long-term strategy will use the latest annual forecast as a starting point.

Annual forecasts differ from monthly forecasts in that the assumptions underlying the previous forecast are completely rethought.

1.6 Top-down and bottom-up forecasts

If a company sells several products or has several divisions, then it will require forecasts of each product or division as well as a forecast for the company as a whole. This raises the problem of whether to use top-down or bottom-up forecasting.

1.6.1 Top-down forecasting

First, a forecast is produced for the company in aggregate from historical company data. Next, individual product or division forecasts are made; then the sum of the forecasts is constrained to add up to the total company forecast. For example, if company sales are forecast to be 90 tonnes next year, but the sum of the product forecasts for next year comes to 100 tonnes, then the product forecasts need to be reduced by an average of 10 per cent in order to sum to 90 tonnes. Usually we reduce each product forecast according to its variability (measured, for example, by its residual standard deviation) rather than by a constant 10 per cent. A procedure to achieve this split of forecast adjustments is known as a *hierarchical analysis*.

The rationale behind the top-down procedure is that product managers will often build excessive optimism into their product forecasts, either to win greater capital sanctions for their product or purely because of human nature. Although each product manager may believe his/her own forecast, few will believe that the sum of all the product forecasts is achievable for the whole company, and the managers will therefore agree to a downgrading of the total company forecast (while each feels that his/her product should be exempt from such a general downgrading!).

1.6.2 Bottom-up forecasting

Here the products or divisions are forecast individually, and then summed to give a total company forecast. This is the traditional method of proceeding. Often the board will be uncomfortable with the resulting total company forecast for the reasons given above, and will make a downward management adjustment to the total without splitting the adjustment into product adjustments. This will lead to a set of 'internal product forecasts', which are the original forecasts provided by the product group, and an 'external company forecast' (including the management adjustment), against which company performance is monitored for the next year.

Because of the inconsistency between internal and external forecasts and in order to avoid over-optimistic forecasts year after year, the top-down method is favoured, and the annual budget review process will be an iterative process in which product forecasts are made, submitted to the board and the planners, revised, resubmitted and so on.

1.7   Forecasting, planning and decision-making

Business forecasts, by themselves, have no function. However, forecasts can be translated into action through the planning process. A forecast is made by considering environmental variables which are either controllable by the company (such as selling price or advertising expenditure) or are not controllable (such as the oil price or the growth of the world economy). Such a forecast can drive a corporate plan which in turn has implications for the decision-makers. These decisions may influence the controllable environmental variables, and thus necessitate an updated forecast which will change the planning assumptions and have further implications for the decision-maker. In other words, forecasting is an *iterative* process.

For example, our initial product forecast may indicate future growth at 10 per cent per annum. Planning on this growth rate indicates the need for new plant in 3 years' time. A decision is taken that current cash flow cannot support capital expenditure for 5 years, so selling prices will be raised to reduce growth and increase cash. A new forecast based on higher selling prices gives growth at 5 per cent p.a., thereby delaying the need to spend money for 5 years. The accompanying cash forecast shows that more cash will be produced than in the high-growth case, and in these circumstances the decision is taken to forgo market share by raising selling prices, and to build new plant after 5 years.

In practice, the decision-making process will be more complicated than this — it will involve profit forecasts as well as volume and cash projections. In addition, the implications for other products cannot be omitted — the future 'shape' of the company has to be right. The advantage of this integrated forecasting and planning process is that it encourages wide participation in the decision-making process. Indeed, a number of inter-departmental meetings will allow this participation to be worked through thoroughly.

Forecasting is an integral part of the day-to-day functioning of a business, and is also a key activity when considering changes in strategy (such as building extra capacity or running a product for cash). However, many companies also employ an annual review of their operations from top to bottom. The idea is to assess how closely the company stuck to its targets during the last year, and to provide new forecasts and targets for the year ahead. Such forecasts are often extended to a time horizon of 3 years in indicative fashion.

Forecasting has been likened to driving a car with a blacked-out front windscreen — the view through the back window provides guidance! To stretch the analogy further, we can assess our current distance from the kerb by looking through the side window, and make appropriate adjustments to our steering in order to get back on course. This is called *monitoring*, and is an important part of the planning process. We cover monitoring and control in Chapter 19.

1.8   Requirements of a good forecast

Since forecasting is just a precursor to planning and decision-making, the usefulness of a forecast relates directly to its 'added value' in making plans or decisions. This concept conflicts with the commonly held belief that a forecast is only useful if it is within certain tight bounds of the actual outcome.

In many decision-making areas the *level* of the forecast variable is of less interest than the *timing* of critical changes to that variable. For example, in order to make a decision about capital expenditure, we need to forecast the *level* of sales over the next 5 years. However, if we are concerned to implement optimal stock levels we need to forecast *changes* in the sales growth rate: in other words, we must forecast the *timing* of peaks and troughs in activity.

We also need to consider the time horizon of the plans to be made. A survival plan requires a short-term forecast, the normal planning cycle works on a medium-term basis, whereas capital-expenditure decisions need to be backed up with long-term forecasts. Good forecasting tools for one time horizon are often indifferent for another.

Our planning needs also dictate how often our forecasts can afford to be 'wrong' while still being useful. On the one hand, we need to be able to predict quality very accurately in an industrial process. On the other hand, a stock-market forecast which successfully predicts whether a share will go up or down with 60 per cent certainty may well be very useful for investment planning.

Again, the different requirements of different forecasts in different areas mean that we need a portfolio of forecasting techniques from which to choose a 'best method' for any given situation. One of the functions of this book is to help to marry up planning situations with suitable forecasting techniques.

The quality of a forecast relates largely to its suitability for planning purposes. However, other factors are also important. A forecast must allow an adequate lead time for a planning response. For example, we may need 3 months' warning of the start of a decline in sales in order to set up leaner stock levels. We need an acceptable level of accuracy, and the cost of carrying out the forecasts must be reasonable. This is particularly true when a lot of forecasts are needed fairly often (for example, in a production process). Finally, it is useful to have a forecasting method which is easy to update when an extra period of data becomes available.

In summary, the quality of a forecast depends on how well it meets the decision needs; adequacy of the lead time to implement policy; statistical accuracy; the cost of the forecast; and ease of updating.

1.9 Broad categories of forecasts

Structured forecasts can be categorized as follows. *Univariate* forecasts depend on past values of the variable to be forecast. *Multivariate* forecasts depend on the past values of a number of other variables. *Deterministic forecasts* depend on relationships which are 'known' (at least to some extent); in other words, statistical estimation is less of a dominant feature than in univariate and multivariate forecasts. Many time-series models fall into the first category, whereas causal models such as econometric methods are to be found in the second.

In addition, we can carry out *eclectic* forecasts where we form a weighted average of

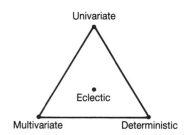

Figure 1.1 The family of forecasts

forecasts from some or all of the above three categories. Armstrong (1978) indicates that eclectic models are often better than single models. Schematically the state space of possible forecasts is the triangle shown in Figure 1.1, with an eclectic forecast anywhere within the triangle (or on one of the sides).

In addition, we can use forecasts which rely totally on 'business experience'. Although business experience is not to be dismissed, the 'gut-feel' forecast is often overrated. As Makridakis (1986) has stated:

> Humans possess unique knowledge and inside information not available to quantitative methods. Surprisingly, however, empirical studies and laboratory experiments have shown that their forecasts are not more accurate than those of quantitative methods. Humans tend to be optimistic and underestimate future uncertainty. In addition the cost of forecasting with judgmental methods is often considerably higher than when quantitative methods are used.

1.10 Summary

The purpose of forecasting relates to the decision-maker's needs via the planning process. The aim is to reduce uncertainty and to give as much information as possible to the decision-maker. Forecasting is a pervasive business activity, and often needs to be drawn together by means of a central department such as the planning department.

We need to forecast macro-economic data, market data and company data. Sometimes we need short-term forecasts, sometimes medium- or long-term projections. Different methods apply to these different cases.

A good forecast will meet the decision needs, give an adequate lead time to implement policy, be accurate, cheap and easy to update. We can choose time-series forecasts, causal forecasts, deterministic forecasts or eclectic forecasts. 'Business experience' is a good adjunct to quantitative forecasting, but should not replace it.

CHAPTER 2

Exploratory data analysis

2.1 Introduction

Many forecasting techniques are statistical in nature. Any statistical analysis is essentially a three-part process, as shown in Figure 2.1. It is tempting to concentrate on the middle element at the expense of the other two. However, we will often obtain misleading results if we do this. This chapter therefore examines how we manage data. Later in the book we will see how to analyze data and how to interpret the results of such analyses. It is just not good enough to be given a data series to forecast, to submit it to a suitable computer package, and to present the printout as the resultant forecast without considering the nature of the data and without interpreting the results.

2.2 Graphing the data

The data we are given may or may not be suitable for immediate analysis. We may need to apply transformations to them, and we will certainly need to choose between a number of competing analytical techniques with which we can treat them.

'Collection of data' in a forecasting context therefore means taking the original series, examining it and applying suitable adjustments to it so that it is in good shape for analysis. An essential first step is to make a simple examination of the data by graphing them. This may appear obvious, but it is all too often omitted in the chase to provide forecasts.

A number of possibilities may present themselves when the data are graphed. We consider each of these in turn.

2.2.1 Stationary data

Figure 2.2 shows a data set which is stationary and well behaved. It is therefore ready for analysis by a procedure designed to deal with stationary series. By saying that the data set is stationary we mean that it is horizontal (that is, it shows no consistent tendency to rise or fall), that its variability is consistent, and that there are no obvious seasonal influences or extreme values. Application of the more sophisticated seasonal adjustment

Figure 2.1   Statistical analysis

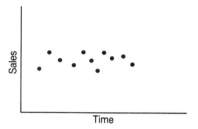

Figure 2.2   A stationary series

routines such as X-11 (see Chapter 20) will test for the significance of both seasonality and extreme values if simple graphing gives an unclear result, but often such tests are unnecessary as the pattern of the data series is clear from the graph.

2.2.2   Non-stationary data

Non-stationary data is the term given to any time series which does not exhibit stationarity. The most common example of this in the business world is sales data incorporating a growth trend, as in Figure 2.3. The trend may be steady or it may vary in slope as time proceeds. Data of this form should either be transformed (see Chapter 13 for details of possible transformations) or be analyzed by a method applicable to non-stationary series.

2.2.3   Discontinuous data

Occasionally a severe shock to the product market will occur. For example, adverse publicity concerning the health risks of a product may cause a sudden reduction in sales. A graph of this type of data will highlight the discontinuity — see, for example, Figure 2.4.

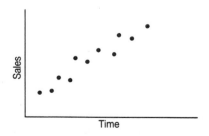

Figure 2.3   Non-stationary data

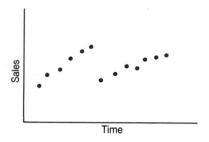

Figure 2.4 Discontinuous data

This kind of data series can either be split into two parts (before the shock and afterwards) and each part analyzed separately, or be analyzed by multiple regression analysis using a dummy variable to differentiate between the two parts. The latter method is only appropriate when the effects of the causal variables remain unchanged before and after the discontinuity. For example, a straight-line model would need to have the same slope before and after the discontinuity in order to use the dummy-variable method. If the slope slackens off after the discontinuity, then it would be necessary to consider the two sections of data separately.

2.2.4 Extreme values

If a data set is well behaved except for one or more 'extreme' points, this will usually be very obvious from graphical inspection (see Figure 2.5). The existence of extreme values can affect statistical analysis radically, especially where the least-squares technique is employed. For this reason it is advisable either to adjust extreme values so that they lie within the variability of the rest of the data, or to treat the values as 'missing values'. Some forecasting tools will carry out this process automatically (for example, the X-11 seasonal adjustment routine), but some require preliminary adjustment of any extreme values before submitting the data to the analysis.

Extreme values will often arise from strikes and will sometimes occur in sequences. For example, the UK hauliers' strike in early 1979 resulted in UK sales figures for many products declining well below trend as the strike took place in January, and then rebounding

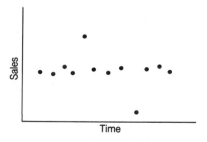

Figure 2.5 Extreme values

well above trend in February and March as depleted stock levels were rebuilt. In this case January, February and March sales needed to be re-estimated by interpolating seasonally adjusted values for December and April (or by a more sophisticated method).

Care also needs to be exercised when carrying out causal analyses. For example, correlating sales with the industrial production index (IPI) would give inaccurate results unless the two data series being correlated had *both* been adjusted for extreme values.

2.2.5 Seasonality

If a data set shows the same pattern within each year — for instance, Quarter 1 is always high, Quarter 3 is alway low — then we have seasonal data as in Figure 2.6. In this case we again have two options. We can either deseasonalize the data using moving averages or X-11, or submit the raw data to a procedure which simultaneously extracts seasonality and forecasts the deseasonalized series. Both of these options are discussed in Chapter 20.

2.2.6 Moving seasonality

Sometimes a time series will exhibit obvious seasonality, but it is equally clear that the seasonal factors for each month or quarter are changing slowly as the years go by (see

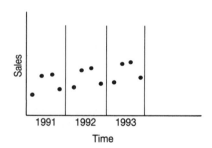

Figure 2.6 Seasonal data

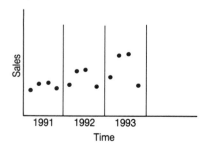

Figure 2.7 Data showing moving seasonality

Figure 2.7). For example, an increasingly long holiday period around Christmas may cause the December seasonal factor to diminish slowly as the years pass (that is, December sales slowly decline as a percentage of total annual sales). A simple seasonal analysis such as the moving average routine only allows for constant seasonality and is therefore inappropriate. Again we can either use X-11, which allows for moving seasonality, or we can employ a method which deseasonalizes allowing for moving seasonality while projecting the deseasonalized data (for example, the Holt—Winters method).

2.2.7 Increasing variance

As sales volume grows it often displays higher variability as in Figure 2.8. For example, data variability will often be proportional to the level of the sales data themselves (that is, variability is a constant percentage of the level of sales). If this is the case then graphing the data will usually make the situation clear. The normal way of dealing with this situation is to transform the data so that it has constant variance. This is necessary because many statistical techniques require constant variance in order to be efficient. An example of a suitable transformation is given in Section 2.3.

2.2.8 Cyclical data

Many sales series are heavily affected by the trade cycle which has a period of several

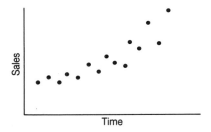

Figure 2.8 Data showing increasing variance

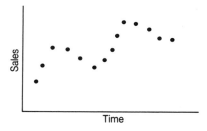

Figure 2.9 Cyclical data

years. (See Chapters 7 and 8 for a full discussion of the trade cycle.) Again this will become clear if the data are graphed as in Figure 2.9. In this case a cyclical model must be used (see Chapter 8 for ways of doing this). If a cyclical model is not used on cyclical data, then the residuals from the non-cyclical model will often be cyclical in nature and cause a number of statistical problems.

2.3   Transformations

Graphing the data can indicate the need for a transformation in order to achieve stationarity, linearity or constant variance. Transformations to achieve constant variance are discussed more fully in Chapter 13.

2.3.1   The logarithmic transformation

Transforming each data point by taking its logarithm will often produce linearity and constant variance in a non-stationary sales series. For example, a sales curve with a constant growth rate will be exponential in nature. By taking logarithms we transform the curve so that it is linear, thereby allowing a simpler model to be fitted (see Figure 2.10). A beneficial and necessary side-effect is often to create constant variance.

Other transformations of this nature are discussed in Chapter 13, and are particularly useful in medium- to long-term forecasting.

2.3.2   Differencing

Differencing aims to detrend data to create stationarity. We create a new series consisting of the differences between adjacent points of the original data. If we call the first difference Δy_t, where y_t is data point number t, then

$$\Delta y_t = y_t - y_{t-1}$$

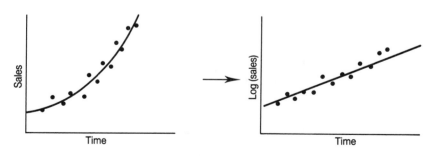

Figure 2.10   The logarithmic transformation

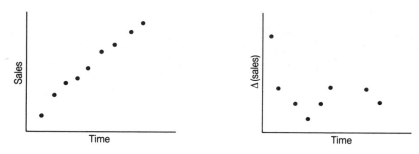

Figure 2.11   Differencing data

Table 2.1   Differenced data shown in Figure 2.11

t	1	2	3	4	5	6	7	8	9
y	2	5	7	8	10	13	15	18	20
Δy		3	2	1	2	3	2	3	1

If the original series can be modelled as a straight line with a non-zero slope, then Δy_t will be stationary, as shown in Figure 2.11 and Table 2.1.

Sometimes we will need to difference data more than once to achieve stationarity. For example, if our data follow a quadratic curve then we will need to difference twice. Denoting a second difference by $\Delta^2 y_t$, we have:

$$\begin{aligned}
\Delta^2 y_t &= \Delta(\Delta y_t) \\
&= \Delta(y_t - y_{t-1}) \\
&= y_t - y_{t-1} - (y_{t-1} - y_{t-2}) \\
&= y_t - 2y_{t-1} + y_{t-2}
\end{aligned}$$

Differencing is particularly useful in detrending data ready for analysis by a short-term stationary model. It will not affect the constancy of variance.

2.3.3   Ratios

Differencing will be inappropriate if the variance increases as the data increase, because in this case the variance of the differences will also increase. A possible remedy for this situation is to create ratios, rather than differences, of successive data points. Denoting the ratio by z_t, we have

$$z_t = y_t / y_{t-1}$$

The ratio is often expressed as a percentage increase of y_t over y_{t-1}. If the differences are proportional to y_t, then the ratios will have a constant variance as required.

A practical complication of both differences and ratios occurs when our original data series is seasonal. In this case creating differences or ratios of successive points will produce a jagged series. For example, suppose that December is seasonally a poor month. Then the difference (ratio) of December to November will normally be negative (less than 100%) whereas the difference (ratio) of January to December will normally be positive (more than 100%). This creates an unwelcome degree of variability in the differenced (ratioed) series. The normal way of eliminating this effect is to take differences (ratios) of every twelfth data point (assuming that we have a monthly series) — that is, we use

$$\Delta y_t = y_t - y_{t-12}$$

or

$$z_t = y_t / y_{t-12}$$

Again we choose between these models according to the constancy of the variance of the series as the data increase.

2.3.4   Trend models

As an alternative to detrending a series in the case of a long-term forecast, we can use trend curve analysis, which will model the trend of the data by means of one of several possible nonlinear trend models. This subject is covered in greater detail in Chapter 9, and, as with many of the techniques described in this book, requires considerable statistical skill. For many 'commodity' products this apparently simplistic procedure works extremely effectively, especially when used in conjunction with cyclical analysis and monitored by residual analysis.

2.4   Measures of forecasting accuracy

After transforming or otherwise adjusting the original data series we will often be able to choose between a number of analyses with which we may provide forecasts. We need some way of selecting the most accurate of these available methods. There are a number of possible measures of forecasting accuracy. These are all functions of the error (or residual) between the actual data and the fitted model.

Denoting the error by e_t, we have

$$e_t = y_t - \hat{y}_t$$

where y_t is data point t and $\hat{y}_t$ is the value fitted by the model for data point t. We can now express the three most popular measures of forecasting accuracy as follows.

The *mean absolute deviation* (MAD) is given by the expression

$$\frac{\Sigma |e_t|}{n}$$

where n is the number of data points. This is simply the average distance between data and forecast.

The *mean squared error* (MSE) is given by

$$\frac{\Sigma e_t^2}{n}$$

and has attractive properties for the statistician, although it penalizes large errors considerably.

The *mean absolute percentage error* (MAPE) is given by

$$\frac{\Sigma(|e_t|/y_t)}{n} \times 100$$

and is the average percentage deviation between data and forecast. As a percentage it is easy to understand, and it is also easy to compare the forecasting accuracy of a method on several different data series.

An example of how we can use these measures is given in Section 2.6.

2.5 Simple short-term forecasting techniques

This section describes two very simple forecasting methods which can be used for making short-term projections. Some more complex techniques which are frequently used in practice can be found in Chapter 5. The purpose behind presenting these two simple methods now is to allow us to consider how to choose between competing forecasting techniques: which one is 'best' for a given set of data?

2.5.1 Naive forecasts

The simplest possible forecast assumes that the most recent data point provides the best information on subsequent points. If we have a data set of n points then the forecast for point $n+1$ is the same as the actual data for point n, i.e.

$$\hat{y}_{t+1} = y_t$$

For example, if the first four weeks' sales for the year have been 34, 42, 38, 46, then our forecast for week 5 is 46.

The naive forecast is often used as a bench-mark: in order to assess the usefulness of another technique we need to ask how much better than the naive method it is. A way of doing this is described later in Section 2.6.

2.5.2 Moving average forecasts

The naive forecast can often work surprisingly well. However, successive forecasts will often jump around considerably for a 'noisy' series. It is more sensible to smooth the trend of such a series and use this smoothed trend to forecast (rather than use the last point which may be obviously rather high or low). Figure 2.12 shows how this trend is likely to provide a less biased estimator of the next data point.

The naive forecast of the next point would be given by the value of point A. However, we may judge that this is an obvious underestimate, and that the value of point B shown on the smoothed trend would be a better estimator. The question is how we calculate the trend. One answer is to evaluate a moving average. For example, instead of forecasting by using the last point, we can calculate the average of the last *three* points and use this as our forecast. This will smooth out the 'noisiness' of the data series:

$$\hat{y}_{t+1} = \tfrac{1}{3}(y_t + y_{t-1} + y_{t-2})$$

For example, if, as before, the first few weeks' sales have been 34, 42, 38, 46 then our forecast for week 5 will be

$\tfrac{1}{3}(42 + 38 + 46) = 42$

Similarly, our forecast for week 4 would have been

$\tfrac{1}{3}(34 + 42 + 38) = 38$

In this particular case the forecast for week 4 is the same as the forecast made by the naive method, whereas the moving average forecast for week 5 is less biased by the apparently extreme value of 46 than the naive forecast.

2.6 Choosing between different forecasting methods

Often a number of competing techniques may be used to forecast a data series. We need to pick the best one for the particular series we have to deal with. In order to do this we use the measures of forecasting accuracy described in Section 2.4.

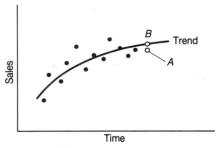

Figure 2.12 Comparison of naive and trend forecasts

As an example we can use a few more weeks of the sales data which we employed in our discussion of the naive and moving average methods of forecasting (Section 2.5). The data are as follows:

34, 42, 38, 46, 36, 32, 40, 36, 44

We can choose between the naive and moving average methods for making forecasts in future by seeing how well they would have forecast within the range of the data. The calculations required to work out the MAD, MSE and MAPE for the naive forecast are shown in Table 2.2. The column marked 'Forecast' shows the forecast which would have been made for any particular week, given the preceding data. For example, the week 5 forecast is 46 (that is, the week 4 actual sales).

From this table we calculate

$$\text{MAD} \quad = \Sigma|e_t|/n \qquad = \frac{54}{8} \quad = 6.75$$

$$\text{MSE} \quad = \Sigma e_t^2/n \qquad = \frac{404}{8} = 50.5$$

$$\text{MAPE} \quad = \frac{\Sigma(|e_t|/y_t)}{n} \qquad = \frac{1.37}{8} = 0.17 \ (= 17\%)$$

We can now repeat the exercise, calculating forecast accuracy for the moving average method. Table 2.3 shows the required calculations. Note that because the moving average forecast needs three data points to make a forecast, we only have projections for weeks 4 to 9. However, this does not matter since all of our measures of accuracy are means.

From the table we calculate

Table 2.2 Naive forecasting accuracy

Week	Sales (y_t)	Forecast $(\hat{y}_t)$	Error $(y_t - \hat{y}_t)$	|Error|	$\frac{\text{\|Error\|}}{y_t}$	Error^2
1	34					
2	42	34	8	8	0.19	64
3	38	42	−4	4	0.11	16
4	46	38	8	8	0.17	64
5	36	46	−10	10	0.28	100
6	32	36	−4	4	0.13	16
7	40	32	8	8	0.20	64
8	36	40	−4	4	0.11	16
9	44	36	8	8	0.18	64
Sum				54	1.37	404

Table 2.3 Moving average forecasting accuracy

Week	Sales (y_t)	Forecast $(\hat{y}_t)$	Error $(y_t - \hat{y}_t)$	$\lvert Error \rvert$	$\dfrac{\lvert Error \rvert}{y}$	$Error^2$
1	34					
2	42					
3	38					
4	46	38	8	8	0.17	64
5	36	42	-6	6	0.17	36
6	32	40	-8	8	0.25	64
7	40	38	2	2	0.05	4
8	36	36	0	0	0.00	0
9	44	36	8	8	0.18	64
Sum				32	0.82	232

$$\text{MAD} \ = \frac{32}{6} \ = 5.33$$

$$\text{MSE} \ = \frac{232}{6} \ = 38.67$$

$$\text{MAPE} \ = \frac{0.82}{6} \ = 0.14 \ (=\ 14\%)$$

Comparing these results with the results for the naive forecast we find that on all three criteria the moving average performs better. For example, the MAPE is only 14 per cent using the moving average, but is 17 per cent using the naive forecast. We would therefore choose to use the moving average forecast in preference to the naive forecast for future projections of this data set.

2.7 Summary

Time-series data need to be carefully screened before they are analyzed. Such screening may highlight the need to transform the data before they can be successfully analyzed. An essential first step is to graph the data.

Graphing the data will give a quick indication of the characteristics of the series. It may be a stationary series or a non-stationary one. In the latter case we can either analyze the data by means of a method suitable for non-stationary series or we can attempt to transform the data to stationarity. Discontinuous data can be split and the two parts analyzed separately or the whole data set may be subjected to a multiple regression analysis with dummy variables. Extreme values can be adjusted or omitted, and seasonality removed or catered for. The data may exhibit non-constant variance, inviting a suitable transformation, and the series may be affected by trade-cycle effects.

Transformations are dealt with in more depth in Chapter 13, but we have seen that the logarithmic transformation is particularly useful, that differencing can be used to detrend data, and that ratios can also be of use in this context. Trend models represent an alternative approach to the problem of detrending long-term data.

The mean absolute deviation, the mean square error and the mean absolute percentage error all measure the accuracy of forecasts. Calculation of these statistics can indicate the best of several potential methods to use on a particular data set.

CHAPTER 3

Residual analysis

3.1 Introduction

Although we have only considered two simple short-term forecasting methods so far, we will defer consideration of other approaches until we have dealt with the interpretation of the results arising from any forecasting technique. A simple but useful procedure is to analyze the residuals or errors created by the forecasting process. For example, we may wish to examine the residuals thrown up by the naive method in Table 2.2 (the column marked 'Error'). Do these residuals indicate that the method we have used is satisfactory? Or is it unsuitable? Alternatively, is it suitable except for the need to include an extra explanatory factor as well? This sort of analysis is called *residual analysis*.

3.2 Residual analysis

3.2.1 Adequate fit

Let us consider the above example. What does residual analysis tell us about the suitability of the naive method for our weekly sales data? The errors or residuals, taken from Table 2.2, are as follows:

   8, −4, 8, −10, −4, 8, −4, 8

Plotting these points, we obtain the graph shown in Figure 3.1

We would expect to have more than eight data values in a real-life example, but this data set will serve to indicate the major points. First, we need to consider time effects. Is there any apparent non-stationary trend in the residuals over the time span considered? This does not appear to be a problem. Second, is the variance of the residuals constant as time proceeds? If the variance increases from left to right then forecasts using this method may be subject to unacceptable variability. Moreover, a changing variance casts doubt on the suitability of the method under consideration. Once more this does not seem to present a problem here. We may, therefore, accept the naive method as an *adequate* short-term forecasting device for these data. This does not mean that it is the *best* method available, as we saw when we compared the forecasting accuracy of the naive and moving

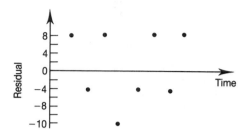

Figure 3.1   Residuals from sales forecast

average methods. Furthermore, we must consider whether a MAPE of 17 per cent is low enough to indicate a satisfactorily precise forecast. If not, then despite having an adequate forecasting method in terms of the pattern of residuals, we may need to look for another more accurate method or to consider extra explanatory variables.

3.2.2   Cyclical terms

A common problem in medium- or longer-term forecasts is the inclusion of cyclical influences. In Chapter 7 we shall consider the effect of the trade cycle on forecasting and planning procedures. The trade cycle is a recurrent sequence of economic booms and periods of depression (low or even negative growth). If our forecasting method fails to account for such cyclical changes then we might expect a residual plot resembling that in Figure 3.2. If we obtain a residual plot like this, it is vital that we modify our forecasting method in order to eliminate the cyclical residuals. Methods for doing this are suggested in Chapter 8.

   Forecasting a cyclical series without accounting for its cyclical nature is clearly unrealistic. Figure 3.3 shows a straight-line forecast which fails to capture the critical features of future performance — the timing and amplitude of future peaks and troughs.

   In practice, of course, the cycle in the original data will probably be masked to some extent by random variation, and it is important under these circumstances to recognize the essential cyclical nature of the data and not to concentrate on the variation. A useful smoothing technique to highlight the cycles is the US Bureau of the Census X-11 seasonal adjustment routine (see Chapter 20), which applies sophisticated smoothing to the data before seasonally adjusting.

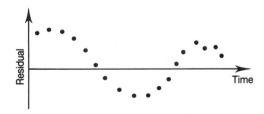

Figure 3.2   Residual plot indicating cyclical movement

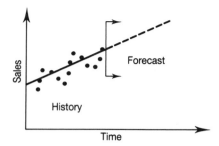

Figure 3.3   Straight-line forecast of a cyclical series

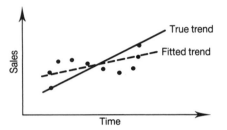

Figure 3.4   Bias in growth rate for a cyclical series

A further reason for ensuring that cyclical effects are adequately modelled is that estimates of growth in product data can be subject to considerable bias if cyclical effects are not picked up. For example, Figure 3.4 shows a cyclical product, and the true growth trend is indicated. However, if we fit a straight line to the data (that is, we ignore the cyclical nature of the series) we will obtain the line marked 'Fitted trend'. The growth rate indicated by this line is quite different from the true growth rate, and this would lead to a forecast which not only omitted the cyclical characteristic of the data, but also projected a biased growth rate for our forecast.

The reason for this is simply that the technique of least squares which we employ in performing a regression analysis will pull the early part of the fitted line up to come as close as possible to the early data, and push the line down later on to try to follow the depressed stage of the cycle as closely as possible.

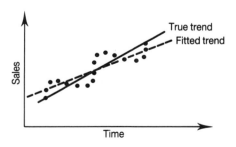

Figure 3.5   Bias in growth rate: longer data set

Of course, we would if possible try to use more than one cycle of data (although often we just do not have more than one cycle, i.e. about five years of data). In this case the bias in our estimate of growth rate would be smaller (see Figure 3.5).

However, the bias can still be considerable, and the maximum error in the span of our data is at the end of the data. This means that our forecast will start off at a considerable distance from the true line, and the bias will increase as we project the forecast further and further. It is difficult enough to forecast as it is, without introducing avoidable bias as well! It is clearly very important to test data and forecasts for cyclical features, even if the product is not thought to be directly cyclical. The trade cycle exists in the overall economy and, as we shall see in Chapter 7, it affects parameters such as interest rates which in turn can influence the sales of apparently non-cyclical products.

3.2.3 Autoregressive error

Figure 3.6 shows a relatively common pattern of residuals in which we see a run of data points to one side of the zero line, rather than a random scattering either side of the line. If this pattern occurs then we have what is known as a *first-order autoregressive* error structure. Reasons for the existence of this sort of effect are discussed in Chapter 13.

We can describe this situation by saying that the error for a particular data point is likely to be close to the error for the previous data point. In statistical notation,

$$e_t = pe_{t-1} + v_t$$

where e_t is the error at time t,

$$|\rho| < 1$$

and

$$v_t \sim N(0, \sigma^2)$$

If $|\rho|$ is close to 1 then we have significant autocorrelation: ρ is known as the *first-order autocorrelation coefficient* and indicates the presence or otherwise of an autoregressive error structure. We need a test to see whether ρ is significantly different from zero. Fortunately such a test exists — it is known as the *Durbin–Watson test*.

3.2.4 The Durbin–Watson test

If our forecasting model generates n residuals e_t, then the Durbin–Watson statistic, d, is given by the following formula:

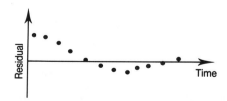

Figure 3.6 First-order autoregressive error

$$d = \frac{\sum_{t=2}^{n}(e_t - e_{t-1})^2}{\sum_{t=1}^{n}e_t^2}$$

Significant values d_U and d_L are tabulated (see Appendix), such that

if $d > d_U$ then ρ is not significantly different from zero;

if $d < d_L$ then ρ is significantly positive;

if $d_L < d < d_U$ then the test is inconclusive.

In the latter case it is probably safest to assume significant autocorrelation and to use one of the methods given below to allow for it.

The tabulated values for the Durbin–Watson statistic depend on the sample size (n) and the number of independent variables in the model (k). For example, if we use a simple regression — say we regress sales on time — then $k = 1$. If our model is a multiple regression model then $k > 1$.

Strictly, the Durbin–Watson statistic tests for positive autocorrelation as defined above. d will lie between 0 and 2. It is possible, though unusual, to test for negative autocorrelation, where successive residuals tend to have opposite signs as in Figure 3.7. In this case d will lie between 2 and 4 and the significant values are $4 - d_U$ and $4 - d_L$, where d_U and d_L are the tabulated values for testing positive autocorrelation. Figure 3.8 indicates areas of significance.

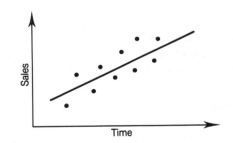

Figure 3.7 Negative autocorrelation

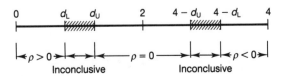

Figure 3.8 Area of significance for the Durbin–Watson statistic

3.2.5   Methods to allow for autoregressive errors

Autoregressive errors are often discovered when using regression models on time series. We then have two options: to retain and modify the regression approach; and to use a different approach.

Retaining the regression approach

We assume here that the high autocorrelation has not arisen as a result of missing out an explanatory variable in the regression equation. It is always worth considering this possibility first.

If we find a high degree of autocorrelation in our errors then it can be unrealistic to project our data using the regression model alone. This is illustrated in Figure 3.9 — the final historical data point is some way from the regression line, and in view of the high degree of autocorrelation in our errors it is highly likely that the first forecast point will lie on the same side of the regression line as the last data point. Continuing this argument beyond the first forecast point, the forecast line is therefore likely to move slowly back to the regression line as indicated in Figure 3.9.

It can be shown that the most likely 'error' $\hat{e}_{t+1}$ from the regression line for the first forecast point is given by

$$\hat{e}_{t+1} = \rho e_t$$

Also, we have

$$\hat{e}_{t+2} = \rho \hat{e}_{t+1} = \rho^2 e_t$$

and, in general,

$$\hat{e}_{t+k} = \rho^k e_t$$

In order to adjust the regression forecast we need an estimate of ρ. This is achieved by calculating the first-order autocorrelation coefficient r_1.

$$r_1 = \frac{\sum_{t=2}^{n} e_t e_{t-1}}{\sum_{t=1}^{n} e_t^2}$$

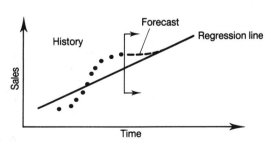

Figure 3.9   Reassessment of a regression forecast in the presence of severe autocorrelation

Let us consider the example of the following data from a 10-year history of sales volume in an industrial product:

Year (t)	1	2	3	4	5	6	7	8	9	10
Sales (y)	21	22.3	23.7	24.5	25.2	25.9	26.7	27.8	29.2	30.5

It is felt for commercial reasons that sales are likely to follow a straight line. What forecasts can we make for the next four years?

Fitting a linear regression to the data we obtain

$$y = 20.29 + 0.979t$$

with a Durbin−Watson statistic of 0.844. Extrapolating the Durbin−Watson table to $n = 10$ we find that this statistic falls below the lower Durbin−Watson critical value for $n = 10$ and $k = 1$, and we therefore have significant autocorrelation which we must account for in our forecast.

Setting $t = 10$, we find that the fitted regression value for the final data point is 30.09. The residual e_{10} is therefore $30.5 - 30.09 = 0.41$. Next we need to determine the autocorrelation coefficient r_1. The calculation is given below, but can be done automatically on many forecasting software packages such as STATGRAPHICS. In this case we have:

$$r_1 = \frac{0.4118}{0.9305}$$
$$= 0.44$$

as shown in Table 3.1.

We must now calculate $\hat{\rho}^k e_{10}$ to find the k-step-ahead forecast. If $\hat{y}$ is the projection from the regression equation, and y_ρ is $\hat{y}$ adapted for the autoregressive error, then we can draw up an adapted regression forecast as in Table 3.2.

Table 3.1   Calculation of autocorrelation

	y	$\hat{y}$	e_1	e_2	$e_1 e_2$	e_1^2
	21	21.27	−0.27			0.0729
	22.3	22.25	0.05	−0.27	−0.0135	0.0025
	23.7	23.23	0.47	0.05	0.0235	0.2209
	24.5	24.21	0.29	0.47	0.1363	0.0841
	25.2	25.19	0.01	0.29	0.0029	0.0001
	25.9	26.16	−0.26	0.01	−0.0026	0.0676
	26.7	27.14	−0.44	−0.26	0.1144	0.1936
	27.8	28.12	−0.32	−0.44	0.1408	0.1024
	29.2	29.10	0.10	−0.32	−0.032	0.01
	30.5	30.08	0.42	0.10	0.042	0.1764
Sum			0.32	−0.37	0.4118	0.9305

Table 3.2   Adapted regression
forecast

t	11	12	13	14
$\hat{y}$	31.06	32.04	33.02	34.00
$\hat{\rho}^{k}e_{10}$	0.22	0.12	0.06	0.03
y_{ρ}	31.28	32.16	33.08	34.03

Autoregressive models

The alternative approach if significant autocorrelation is present is to use an autoregressive model. The most sophisticated forecasting scheme which includes autoregressive models as a subset is known as *Box—Jenkins forecasting*. This is a time-series approach rather than a causal model and is heavily dependent on the experience of the practitioner. For a short discussion of the Box—Jenkins approach, see Chapter 6.

3.2.6   Sensitivity analysis

In Chapter 2 we saw how to assess the suitability of a forecasting model for a particular data set by measuring either the MAD, MSE or MAPE. This procedure measures how accurately the model fits the data. However, our data set is in the form of a time series, and we really need a measure which tests how *stable* the forecast is as time progresses.

For example, suppose we fit a straight line to a data set which is quadratic in nature, as in Figure 3.10. A forecast based on the first four points is clearly going to be lower than a forecast based on all eight points. As more and more points are added to the model, the forecast line will develop a higher and higher slope. The forecast is clearly unstable and an alternative model should be sought.

This idea of considering model forecasts based on successive subsets of the data is known as *sensitivity analysis*. It has the advantages of highlighting model instability and of giving an indication of likely confidence limits for any forecasts made. These confidence limits are likely to be wider than the theoretical confidence limits arising from the model alone,

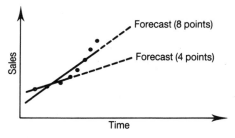

Figure 3.10   Sensitivity analysis

and reflect the fact that actual confidence limits in practical forecasting are invariably far wider than theoretical confidence limits would imply.

The following example demonstrates how to use sensitivity analysis. We have eight data points to which we aim to fit a simple linear regression. We fit simple regressions to the first five, six, seven and eight points successively, giving the forecast lines and forecasts of point 9 as shown in Figure 3.11. We can now plot the successive values of $\hat{y}_9$ against the number of data points used in the model (Figure 3.12).

We notice that $\hat{y}_9$ increases as time progresses, so we are suspicious that any forecast may underestimate what is likely to transpire. This indicates that the model is unsuitable. Either a nonlinear model is needed, or a logarithmic transformation should be considered. A satisfactory pattern of residuals would be independently and identically distributed with no autocorrelation. If there *is* autocorrelation then we must fit an autoregressive model, as ordinary least squares will give incorrect results.

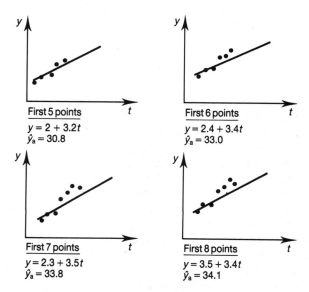

First 5 points
$y = 2 + 3.2t$
$\hat{y}_a = 30.8$

First 6 points
$y = 2.4 + 3.4t$
$\hat{y}_a = 33.0$

First 7 points
$y = 2.3 + 3.5t$
$\hat{y}_a = 33.8$

First 8 points
$y = 3.5 + 3.4t$
$\hat{y}_a = 34.1$

Figure 3.11   Sensitivity analysis: linear model

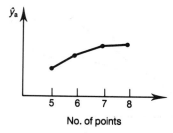

No. of points

Figure 3.12   Sensitivity graph

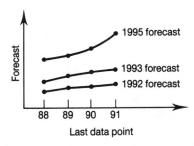

Figure 3.13 Multiple sensitivity analysis

Sensitivity analyses can be carried out for a number of time periods ahead. This can assess the shorter- and longer-term sensitivity of a forecast — for more complicated forecasting methods these sensitivities may be different. Figure 3.13 shows a sensitivity analysis for 1-, 2- and 4-year-ahead forecasts.

3.3   Out-of-sample fitting

So far we have chosen which of a range of models to use on a particular data set by fitting each model to the whole span of the data; calculating the MAD, MSE or MAPE for each model; and choosing the model which provides the lowest MAD, MSE or MAPE. This is known as *in-sample fitting* and chooses the model which best fits historical data. However, we are in the business of forecasting, and it would therefore be preferable to choose the model which forecasts future data best rather than the one which fits past data best. Unfortunately, future data are always lacking! Luckily, we can adapt our circumstances and generate 'future data' quite easily. Suppose we have 12 years of data. In-sample fitting would involve fitting various competing models to all 12 points and looking for the smallest MSE (say). However, we could pretend that we only possess the first eight data points and that the remaining four are unknown. We can then fit our models to the eight available data points and calculate their MSEs over the final ('future') four points. This is known as *out-of-sample fitting*. Figures 3.14 and 3.15 indicate the procedure for choosing between different models.

Let us consider a simple illustrative example. Annual sales volume at Downwell Buckets for the last 12 years has been as follows:

3 5 9 13 17 22 28 32 35 37 36 37

A linear model has been suggested to forecast this series. As an alternative, a quadratic model may well follow the apparently nonlinear growth trend better. Which model is preferable using, first, in-sample fitting, and second, out-of-sample fitting? How would you forecast this series in practice?

Denoting time in years as t, we can fit a linear regression to all 12 points (in-sample fitting). The results of this are to produce the fitted line

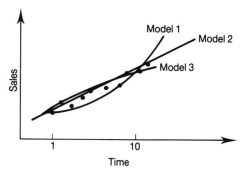

$\hat{y}_t = f(y_1, ..., y_{10})$ for each model

$$MSE = \frac{\sum\limits_{t=1}^{10} (y_t - \hat{y}_t)^2}{10} \quad \text{for each model}$$

Choose model with minimum MSE

Figure 3.14   In-sample fitting

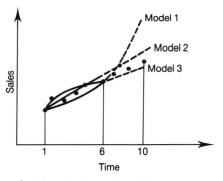

$\hat{y}_t = f(y_1, ..., y_6)$ for each model

$$MSE = \frac{\sum\limits_{t=7}^{10} (y_t - \hat{y}_t)^2}{4} \quad \text{for each model}$$

Choose model with minimum MSE

Figure 3.15   Out-of-sample fitting

Sales $= -0.12 + 3.53t$

with an MSE of 7.02. Similarly, we can fit a quadratic curve which results in the line

Sales $= -5.55 + 5.86t - 0.18t^2$

with an MSE of 3.47.

Apparently the quadratic curve fits better over the length of the data and would therefore be chosen, especially as the MSE has been halved compared with the linear case. As an aside, however, it is worth commenting that the use of a quadratic curve for long-term forecasting is usually a recipe for disaster, because all quadratics have turning points which can easily lead to predictions of negative sales!

We now drop the last four points from the data series, leaving us with eight points of historical data. Fitting the linear model to our eight points (out-of-sample fitting) gives the following fitted equation:

Sales $= -3.21 + 4.30t$

A quadratic model fitted to the same eight points gives

Sales $= -0.09 + 2.42t + 0.21t^2$

We can now predict points 9 to 12 using each of these equations in turn. By taking the mean of the squares of the residuals we can also obtain an MSE for each model. These calculations are shown in Table 3.3.

On an out-of-sample basis it is clear that the linear model is vastly superior, thus reversing the decision made on the basis of in-sample fitting. This lack of correlation between the results of in-sample and out-of-sample fitting is not unusual, and in the interests of choosing the model which gives the best forecasting performance (rather than the best fitting performance) it is a good idea to use the out-of-sample criterion whenever possible.

Another point worth noting is that the MSEs estimated by the out-of-sample methodology are far larger than those derived from in-sample fitting. Again this is a common result, and underlines why confidence limits calculated from in-sample methods usually underestimate the forecast variability which is likely to arise in practice.

Finally, one has to ask whether one would use *either* of these forecast models. A sensitivity analysis would highlight instability in both forecasts, leading to the conclusion that neither model is satisfactory. Had we taken the trouble to graph the data in the first place, it would have become fairly clear that a long-term trend curve (such as the gompertz) would have stood a better chance of forecasting the data well. Trend curves are covered in Chapter 9. Again if we want to test the forecasting performance of the gompertz on this data, we would use the out-of-sample methodology to generate an MSE, together with a sensitivity analysis to test stability.

Clearly we need to make a sensible split in our data between history and 'future' — we need enough data points to estimate the competing models with a reasonable degree of accuracy, but we also need enough forecast points to generate a meaningful MSE. The

Table 3.3 Out-of-sample MSE calculations

Point	Sales	Linear forecast	Residual squared	Quadratic forecast	Residual squared
9	35	35.5	0.25	38.6	12.96
10	37	39.8	7.84	45.0	64.00
11	36	44.1	65.61	51.8	249.64
12	37	48.4	129.96	59.0	484.00
MSE			50.92		202.65

usual rule of thumb is to use about two-thirds of the data as history, leaving the other third as 'forecast'

3.4 Summary

Residual analysis can test whether a particular forecasting method is suitable for a particular data set. It can highlight an adequate fit, the presence of unexplained cyclical terms, and the presence of autoregressive errors. If the latter condition is suspected, then it can be tested by the Durbin–Watson statistic. If this demonstrates significant autocorrelation then two approaches to the problem can be pursued. Either the original model (often a regression model) can be retained and the forecasts modified, or the Box–Jenkins approach can be adopted, although this is a model which many find somewhat complicated.

Sensitivity analysis is a useful way of assessing the stability of forecasts provided by any particular model as more and more data points are added. It indicates models which might give systematic bias and often leads to data transformation and/or the use of different methodology. It also gives an insight into practical confidence limits which are often a lot wider than theory would imply.

Out-of-sample fitting shows which of a number of competing models is likely to forecast best. In-sample fitting shows which model fits the data best. In the interests of obtaining the best forecasting model it is therefore advisable to use out-of-sample fitting wherever possible.

CHAPTER 4

Dirty data

A major problem in forecasting is concerned with data which are less precise than they appear. We can dub this as the problem of *dirty data*. Unfortunately, forecasting models are subject to the same laws as any other type of model, in particular the garbage in— garbage out (GIGO) principle. All too often we ascribe rather greater accuracy to our forecasting models than they deserve because some of the data on which they are built are of dubious quality. This chapter details a number of areas in which dirty data can proliferate. In particular, we examine the difficulties involved in using statistics such as the industrial production index as explanatory variables in regression models. The aim is not to discourage the reader, rather to sound a warning.

4.1 Product sector data

We will often want to use data for the whole of a production sector. For example, we may have a chemical product which we wish to forecast with reference to the total output of the chemicals sector. Let us suppose that we sell our product into three European markets. Chemical production data for the three countries concerned are available from relevant government publications. However, the make-up of chemical production in one country may not be the same as in another country. For example, in some countries chemical production includes production of fibres, and in others it does not. Similar discrepancies exist with respect to oil refining and rubber products, which may or may not be included in total chemical production. In addition, production in some product areas may be split between two or more major sectors. An example of this is plastics production, which falls under chemical production in the UK, while plastics processing does not. It is, therefore, important to be vigilant and to understand the hierarchy of products which make up the higher-level production indices in the various countries of interest.

4.2 Sector definitions from different sources

There are several organizations which provide production and other data by country — among them the UN, OECD and EC. Unfortunately, using country data from such sources still presents difficulties, since they all use slightly different definitions. For example, it can be dangerous to compare chemical production for one country from one source with chemical production for another country from a second source. There is no available data base which deals with all countries at all levels of aggregation, so that using a number of different sources must involve careful consideration of the relevant sector definitions.

4.3   Merchanted goods

Many companies 'sell on' goods. Typically, in times of product shortage a company may buy another company's product to sell on to its customers. A company will often be willing to stand a loss in engaging in selling on, if in so doing it is able to keep an attractive customer on its books. Unfortunately, selling on can result in double-counting in production statistics as both companies may report a sale (on which initial production statistics are based). Substantial selling on, which may occur at times of peak business activity, is therefore likely to inflate production indices at that time.

A similar activity involves the double-counting of intra-company sales. A company may have two divisions, one of which sells an intermediate product to the other. The second division puts the intermediate product through a manufacturing process before selling the resulting product to a customer. It is important that the company does not double-count the sales made by the two divisions, and that intra-company sales are stripped out of any total company production statistics.

4.4   Provision of government statistics

Government statistics are processed by relatively junior staff, and the data provided by companies are also dealt with by junior company staff. This increases the possibility of error in comparison, for example, with sector federation statistics (see Section 4.11). In addition, government sources are slow to change company definitions in order to reflect changing production patterns. For example, many of the ICI product definitions date back to the formation of the company in 1926! Provision of statistics invariably follows 'previous practice'. In addition, production statistics will tend to include capital sales due, for example, to the sale of company offices.

4.5   Geographical classification

It would be nice to think that the geography of the world is not still under discussion. Unfortunately, this appears not so. Some publications assign Mexico's business statistics to North America, some to South America. Some place Turkey in Europe and some in Asia. Some classify Turkey as an undeveloped country, some as a developing country. In carrying out business analyses and forecasts for geographical aggregates it is important to ensure that these aggregates are consistently named and defined.

4.6 Prices

Much business forecasting and planning involves production or market statistics. However, prices are also important due to their close relationship with profits. It is again sensible to tread carefully in this area.

For example, producer prices are the average prices of home-based production only, whereas wholesale prices involve prices of home-based material plus imports. Which index is the more useful is dependent on the context of the study being undertaken. Again these two price indices are quoted by most countries, but the definition differs from country to country. A second problem area is the question of whether indices or prices themselves involve list prices or actual prices. List prices are used in the make-up of various statistics and are not, therefore, a sensible guide to profitability. Discounts from list price are often substantial and move markedly from month to month: this behaviour is not reflected in price indices based on list prices — these often tend to be fairly flat through the year before showing a sizeable upturn on 1 January. The treatment of price indices and the prevalence of list pricing differ considerably between sectors. Finally, it is important to be aware of whether prices include freight and insurance charges (that is, whether they are f.o.b. or c.i.f.). Consistency is the key.

4.7 Trade statistics

When considering market data we often wish to add or subtract net exports or net imports of a product. Unfortunately, trade statistics are notoriously unreliable. Figures on exports and imports are collected on different bases, and the difference between the world's exports and its imports, which should be zero, will often be as high as $100 billion — roughly 3—4 per cent of world trade. To make matters worse, this difference is not a constant factor, but varies wildly from year to year. As a result, it is important to be careful of trade statistics and to use the most reliable source available (often sector federation data).

4.8 The single European market

One of the advantages of the changes instigated in 1992 will be common definitions in country statistics within Europe. Reclassification will cause transitional problems as definitions are changed and long runs of consistent data are no longer available, but against that must be set the improvement which will be made to inter-country comparisons.

4.9 Indices

There are two types of problem associated with indices. These are problems arising from rebasing and revision of such data.

Rebasing is normally carried out every 5 years and allows the statistics to reflect changing weightings of the products which make up the index. Problems occur typically when prices move around rapidly for a particular class of products. For example, rebasing of Japanese output indices in 1985 gave rise to a 3 per cent upward revision of volume and a 3 per cent downward revision of prices due to the fall in oil prices between 1980 and 1985. Therefore, any regression analyses using the output indices as dependent variables prior to 1985 would have required reanalysis to take into account the revised data.

Revisions, on the other hand, are month-to-month changes of data independent of rebasing revisions. For example, production indices are estimated initially by sampling the total population of companies in the sector. However, as more and more hard information becomes available as the months pass the initial estimates can change radically. It is not unknown for major production sector data to change by 7–8 per cent in the course of the year after initial publication. Revisions continue for up to 10 years although the changes become smaller as time proceeds. The extent of this problem indicates the difficulty of using up-to-date data in regression analyses, the parameters of which can need substantial re-estimation when final data become available. Variables which appear significant at first may lose their significance when revised data are used.

4.10 Volume

Production volume can be estimated by using added value or an add-up of the tonnages of the products concerned. The practice differs from country to country. This is an important feature to clarify — for example, it may be entirely inappropriate to construct tonnage-based indices if radically different products are involved.

4.11 Industry federation statistics

As we have observed, there is an alternative to government-produced indices in many areas. In the search for reliable statistics, many industries have set up central bodies whose duties include the collection of production, market, price and trade statistics particular to them. These bodies can either be country-based or continent-based. Examples of the latter are CEFIC, which produces chemical industry statistics, and FIDES, which supplies plastics data, both for the European market, by country. They are neutral bodies which respect the confidentiality of the company data they collect. They collate the data and send back the totals to the member companies.

Such bodies achieve a wide coverage of their markets because of the value which member companies place on reliable data. Since the member companies will use the aggregated data extensively they take more care in producing these statistics than they do for inputs to government statistics. As a result, this approach yields more accurate data more quickly than is the case with government statistics. They are less subject to revision than government statistics, although occasional definitional revisions are necessary which require re-estimation of back data.

4.12 Summary

1. Government or international organizations' statistics need to be examined carefully before use. Country and product definitions can differ considerably between the data agencies.
2. Many statistics are unreliable because of collection methods and definitional problems. There is often little that can be done about this situation.
3. Indices are often revised heavily and rebasing can cause apparent step changes. Extreme caution is needed when carrying out regression analyses using recent data of this sort.
4. Industry statistics produced by industry federations are usually much more reliable than government statistics and should be used wherever possible.
5. As a result of the prevalence of 'dirty data':
    (i) use good-quality data wherever possible — the quality range is large.
    (ii) use data which are *counted* rather than *estimated* wherever possible. For example, use demographic statistics in preference to production indices in a regression equation.
    (iii) the prevalence of 'dirty data' will inflate theoretical confidence limits considerably. Be realistic in this area.
    (iv) weight recent data more heavily than data from long ago which may have definitional incompatibilities. But beware of index number revisions.
    (v) do not dodge the pain of collecting high-quality data. Do not underestimate the time and expert knowledge needed to do this.

CHAPTER 5

Short-term forecasting 1

One-step-ahead forecasts

5.1 Introduction

We now consider forecasting various lengths of time ahead. This chapter describes some
of the more popular methods of short-term forecasting, which usually means up to 12
months ahead. Later chapters will be concerned with medium-term forecasting (1−3 years
ahead) and long-term forecasting (over 3 years ahead). As we shall see, different methods
are needed as our time perspective changes. There is no magic method which can do a
good job regardless of time horizon.

It has been shown empirically that simple methods often work as well as more complex
methods. We will therefore prefer such techniques, and in doing so we will follow the
preferences of the business world, where user-friendliness and ease of use are powerful
selling points, rather than those of the academic world. In this book we aim to reflect
current business practice, not current academic practice.

All the methods in this chapter are easily computerized, and can be run automatically,
quickly and cheaply. They are, therefore, ideal for applications where many regular
forecasts need to be provided — for example, stock control over an extensive grade range.

5.2 Methods for data without trend

5.2.1 The naive method

The simplest possible method is the naive method. This says that the forecast for the next
time period is the same as the actual datum for this time period. In statistical notation:

$$\hat{y}_{t+1} = y_t$$

An example of the naive method was given in Chapter 2. It forms the bench-mark against
which other forecasting methods are assessed. We might expect that any reasonably
sophisticated method would outperform the naive method by a considerable margin, but
in practice this is not the case, and the degree by which any given method outperforms
the naive method is well worth estimating. Makridakis *et al.* (1982) performed experiments

to assess the relative accuracy of various methods when applied to practical data sets, and came to valuable and interesting conclusions as to the unexpectedly good accuracy of fairly simple models compared with the more sophisticated methods available.

5.2.2 Moving averages

The naive forecast suffers from volatility when operating with a 'noisy' series. To counteract this tendency, it is sensible to try to extract the short-term trend from the data, and to extend this trend. We can do this by smoothing the data with a moving average. A simple n-point moving average is expressed in statistical notation as follows:

$$\hat{y}_{t+1} = \frac{1}{n}(y_t + y_{t-1} + y_{t-2} + \ldots + y_{t-n+1})$$

An example was given in Chapter 2 of a 3-point moving average.

5.2.3 Exponential smoothing

Simple moving averages smooth the data, but weight each point equally. We may well feel that we wish to apply more weight to the most recent points and less weight to data from a longer time ago. One way to achieve this aim is to use *exponential* smoothing. With this method we employ a moving average of infinite length and with gradually decreasing weighting. The formula is as follows:

$$\hat{y}_{t+1} = \alpha y_t + (1-\alpha)\hat{y}_t, \quad 0 \leq \alpha \leq 1 \tag{5.1}$$

so that the forecast for $t+1$, $\hat{y}_{t+1}$, depends not only on y_t but also on the forecast made for time t. The value of α can be chosen to apply a lesser or greater degree of smoothing. Note that the case of $\alpha = 1$ gives us the naive method with no smoothing.

Expanding equation (5.1) we obtain

$$\hat{y}_{t+1} = \alpha y_t + \alpha(1-\alpha)y_{t-1} + (1-\alpha)^2\hat{y}_{t-1}$$

and we can continue expanding this expression to give the following:

$$\hat{y}_{t+1} = \alpha y_t + \alpha(1-\alpha)y_{t-1} + \alpha(1-\alpha)^2 y_{t-2} + \alpha(1-\alpha)^3 y_{t-3} + \ldots \tag{5.2}$$

which demonstrates that equation (5.1) is equivalent to a moving average of infinite length with decreasing weights as required.

The weight α is usually chosen so that $0.1 \leq \alpha \leq 0.3$. For example, if $\alpha = 0.1$ then successive coefficients in equation (5.2) are

0.1, 0.09, 0.081, 0.0729, 0.065 61, ...

To take the other extreme, if $\alpha = 0.9$ then the coefficients are

0.9, 0.09, 0.009, 0.0009, 0.000 09, ...

Table 5.1 shows the world-wide sales of a chemical product for the years 1985 and 1986. The data have already been seasonally adjusted and a forecast is required for 1987.

Table 5.1 Exponential smoothing:
$\alpha = 0.1$

Period	Data	Forecast	Error	Error^2
1	99.8	99.80		
2	98.4	99.80	−1.40	1.96
3	98.6	99.66	−1.06	1.12
4	98.7	99.55	−0.85	0.73
5	101.7	99.47	2.23	4.98
6	98.0	99.69	−1.69	2.86
7	102.4	99.52	2.88	8.28
8	100.5	99.81	0.69	0.48
9	99.3	99.88	−0.58	0.34
10	101.2	99.82	1.38	1.90
11	102.7	99.96	2.74	7.51
12	98.9	100.23	−1.33	1.78
13	104.5	100.10	4.40	19.36
14	101.9	100.54	1.36	1.85
15	91.5	100.68	−9.18	84.20
16	117.5	99.76	17.74	314.77
17	102.9	101.53	1.37	1.87
18	106.2	101.67	4.53	20.53
19	107.0	102.12	4.88	23.79
20	108.3	102.61	5.69	32.37
21	108.6	103.18	5.42	29.39
22	112.5	103.72	8.78	77.07
23	106.4	104.60	1.80	3.24
24	128.6	104.78	23.82	567.43
Forecast		107.16		
Mean square error				52.51

Table 5.1 illustrates the derivation of a forecast by exponential smoothing. A value of 0.1 is taken for α. The initial forecast for period 1 is assumed to be the same as the data for point 1: 99.8. Using equation (5.2) the second forecast point is derived as

$$\hat{y}_2 = 0.1 \times 99.8 + 0.9 \times 99.8$$
$$= 99.8$$

The third forecast point, using the same equation, is

$$\hat{y}_3 = 0.1 \times 98.4 + 0.9 \times 99.8$$
$$= 99.66$$

The forecast for point 25 is

$$\hat{y}_{25} = 0.1 \times 128.6 + 0.9 \times 104.78$$
$$= 107.16$$

The forecast for points 26, 27, 28, ... is also 107.16 since we are assuming that there is no trend in the data.

The mean square error is 52.51, a value which is heavily inflated by points 16 and 24, both of which exhibit unusually high sales. This is not at all an unusual occurrence in real-life data series, and a decision needs to be taken as to whether to test for outliers and modify the offending points if significant outliers are detected. Since point 15 is low and point 16 is high it is possible that a plant problem curtailed sales in period 15 and that some catching-up was achieved in period 16. The high value in period 24 looks like a December in which the normal seasonal downturn did not materialize. Unfortunately, since point 24 is the last point of the data it causes a step change in the forecast for point 25 and for subsequent points. The cause of this upturn needs to be found so that we can determine whether the forecast level is reasonable.

In this case we have used an α-value of 0.1. We could have used any value of α between 0 and 1. In order to determine the optimum value of α, we need to recalculate Table 5.1 using different values. We can then choose the value of α which minimizes the MSE of the one-step-ahead forecasts. Table 5.1 shows that for $\alpha = 0.1$ we obtain an MSE of 52.51. Table 5.2 shows the same forecast using $\alpha = 0.3$: this yields an MSE of 43.61. On the

Table 5.2 Exponential smoothing: $\alpha = 0.3$

Period	Data	Forecast	Error	Error^2
1	99.8	99.80		
2	98.4	99.80	−1.40	1.96
3	98.6	99.38	−0.78	0.61
4	98.7	99.15	−0.45	0.20
5	101.7	99.01	2.69	7.22
6	98.0	99.82	−1.82	3.31
7	102.4	99.27	3.13	9.78
8	100.5	100.21	0.29	0.08
9	99.3	100.30	−1.00	1.00
10	101.2	100.00	1.20	1.44
11	102.7	100.36	2.34	5.48
12	98.9	101.06	−2.16	4.67
13	104.5	100.41	4.09	16.70
14	101.9	101.64	0.26	0.07
15	91.5	101.72	−10.22	104.39
16	117.5	98.65	18.85	355.24
17	102.9	104.31	−1.41	1.98
18	106.2	103.88	2.32	5.36
19	107.0	104.58	2.42	5.86
20	108.3	105.31	2.99	8.97
21	108.6	106.20	2.40	5.74
22	112.5	106.92	5.58	31.11
23	106.4	108.60	−2.20	4.82
24	128.6	107.94	20.66	426.96
Forecast		114.14		
Mean square error				43.61

basis of these two runs we would choose to produce forecasts using $\alpha = 0.3$. In practice we would run the model for several values of α in order to obtain a more precise estimate of the optimum value.

5.3 Methods for data with trend

5.3.1 Brown's method

The method which we have called exponential smoothing is more accurately called *single* exponential smoothing. It works well if the data have no medium- to long-term trend. However, production or sales data usually exhibit an upward trend, and if we apply single exponential smoothing (SES) to it, our forecasts will tend to fall below the out-turn since we are deriving our forecast from weighted values of past (that is, lower) data (see Figure 5.1). Brown's method utilizes exponential smoothing while making an allowance for the trend in the data.

As we can see from Figure 5.1, single exponential smoothing provides forecasts which fall a certain amount below the actual data on average. Let us suppose that this underestimate averages some constant k. If we carry out a further single exponential smoothing on the smoothed data we obtain a doubly smoothed series which will fall on average an amount k below the SES series. This process is known as *double exponential smoothing* (DES). We therefore have the original series with the SES series on average k below it, and the DES series a further k below the SES (see Figure 5.2).

Brown's method estimates forecasts for the data within the sample by noting that the data are approximately given by the value of the SES plus k (which can be estimated by $SES - DES$). Therefore the in-sample forecast is given by

$$y = 2 \times SES - DES$$

To obtain an *m*-step-ahead forecast beyond the end of the data we take our forecast for y and add m times an estimate for the slope of the line. This slope can be shown to be given by

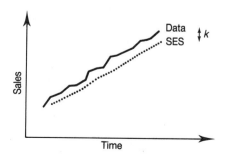

Figure 5.1 Single exponential smoothing of data with a trend

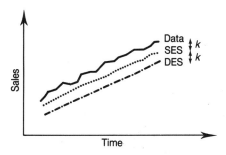

Figure 5.2 Double exponential smoothing of data with a trend

$$b = \frac{\alpha}{1-\alpha}(SES - DES)$$

The full set of equations to carry out Brown's method and provide an m-step-ahead forecast is as follows:

$$S_t' = \alpha y_y + (1-\alpha)S_{t-1}' \qquad \text{(5.3) (SES)}$$

$$S_t'' = \alpha S_t' + (1-\alpha)S_{t-1}'' \qquad \text{(5.4) (DES)}$$

$$a_t = 2S_t' - S_t'' \qquad \text{(5.5)}$$

$$b_t = \frac{\alpha}{1-\alpha}(S_t' - S_t'') \qquad \text{(5.6)}$$

$$\hat{y}_{t+m} = a_t + mb_t \qquad \text{(5.7)}$$

where S_t' gives single-smoothed and S_t'' double-smoothed data, a_t the in-sample forecast, b_t the slope, and $\hat{y}_{t+m}$ is the m-step-ahead forecast.

For example, Table 5.3 shows a forecast of the world-wide sales of the same chemical product as was used in Table 5.1. Points 1 to 24 relate to the months of the years 1981 and 1982. All data have been seasonally adjusted. The forecasts are built up as follows.

For $t = 1$,

$$S_1' = S_1'' = 78.2.$$

This is the starting value for both SES and DES series. It equals the first data point.

For $t = 2$,

$$\begin{aligned} S_2' &= 0.3 \times 78.6 + 0.7 \times 78.2 \\ &= 78.32 \end{aligned}$$

using equation (5.3) with $\alpha = 0.3$. Also,

$$\begin{aligned} S_2'' &= 0.3 \times 78.32 + 0.7 \times 78.2 \\ &= 78.24 \end{aligned}$$

using equation (5.4). Then

$$\begin{aligned} a_2 &= 2 \times 78.32 - 78.24 \\ &= 78.40 \end{aligned}$$

Table 5.3 Brown's method: $\alpha = 0.3$

Period	Data	Smoothed data	Double smoothed	$a(t)$	$b(t)$	Forecast	Error
1	78.2	78.20	78.20				
2	78.6	78.32	78.24	78.40	0.04		
3	80.2	78.88	78.43	79.34	0.19	78.44	−1.76
4	81.6	79.70	78.81	80.59	0.38	79.53	−2.07
5	77.6	79.07	78.89	79.25	0.08	80.97	3.37
6	84.1	80.58	79.40	81.76	0.51	79.33	−4.77
7	78.5	79.95	79.56	80.35	0.17	82.27	3.77
8	83.7	81.08	80.02	82.14	0.45	80.51	−3.19
9	85.6	82.43	80.74	84.13	0.73	82.59	−3.01
10	85.2	83.26	81.50	85.03	0.76	84.85	−0.35
11	84.5	83.64	82.14	85.13	0.64	85.79	1.29
12	80.4	82.66	82.30	83.03	0.16	85.77	5.37
13	82.5	82.62	82.39	82.84	0.10	83.19	0.69
14	81.8	82.37	82.39	82.36	−0.01	82.93	1.13
15	86.0	83.46	82.71	84.21	0.32	82.35	−3.65
16	82.4	83.14	82.84	83.45	0.13	84.53	2.13
17	83.4	83.22	82.95	83.49	0.11	83.58	0.18
18	85.9	84.02	83.27	84.77	0.32	83.60	−2.30
19	85.3	84.41	83.61	85.20	0.34	85.09	−0.21
20	84.1	84.31	83.82	84.81	0.21	85.54	1.44
21	88.1	85.45	84.31	86.59	0.49	85.02	−3.08
22	84.0	85.02	84.52	85.51	0.21	87.08	3.08
23	84.9	84.98	84.66	85.30	0.14	85.72	0.82
24	86.5	85.44	84.89	85.98	10.23	85.44	−1.06
25						86.21	
26						86.45	
27						86.68	
28						86.91	
29						87.14	
30						87.38	
31						87.61	
32						87.84	
33						88.08	
34						88.31	
35						88.54	
36						88.77	

Mean absolute error	1.78
Mean absolute percentage error	2.12
Mean square error	5.23
Mean error	0.36
(all for time periods 10−24)	

using equation (5.5), and

$$b_2 = \frac{0.3}{0.7}(78.32 - 78.24)$$
$$= 0.04$$

using equation (5.6). Therefore the forecast for point 3 is

$$\hat{y}_3 = 78.40 + 0.04$$
$$= 78.44$$

using equation (5.7) with $m = 1$. These calculations are repeated to provide one-step-ahead forecasts up to period 24. The m-step-ahead forecasts are now estimated using equation (5.7). Thus

$$\hat{y}_{25} = 85.98 + 0.23 = 86.21$$
$$\hat{y}_{26} = 85.98 + 0.23 \times 2 = 86.45$$
$$\hat{y}_{27} = 85.98 + 0.23 \times 3 = 86.68$$

and so on.

Values of the parameter α between 0.1 and 0.3 are commonly used.

5.3.2 Holt's method

Brown's method retains the attractions of exponential smoothing while allowing for a trend in the data. It uses just one parameter, α, to model both the level of the series and the slope of the line. To allow more flexibility we could use two parameters — one for the level of the series and one for the slope. Holt's method uses this idea while retaining exponential smoothing methodology. We use two parameters, α and γ, and employ single exponential smoothing for both level and trend. Our m-step-ahead forecast is the latest estimate of the level plus m times the latest estimate of the slope. The equations are as follows:

$$S_t = \alpha y_t + (1-\alpha)(S_{t-1} + b_{t-1}) \qquad (5.8)$$
$$b_t = \gamma(S_t - S_{t-1}) + (1-\gamma)b_{t-1} \qquad (5.9)$$
$$\hat{y}_{t+m} = S_t + mb_t \qquad (5.10)$$

Equation (5.8) gives the current level of the series, equation (5.9) the current value of the trend, and equation (5.10) gives the forecast. Note that adding b_{t-1} in equation (5.8) corrects S_{t-1} for the growth seen between times $t-1$ and time t. Also, the term $S_t - S_{t-1}$ in equation (5.9) estimates the growth rate between times $t-1$ and t.

Both Brown's method and Holt's method perform well in practice, with Holt's method generally the more accurate, although there is often little difference between them. Indeed, it can be shown that Brown's method is a special case of Holt's method. Unfortunately, starting values are critical; comments on how to handle this are made in the following example.

Table 5.4 shows Holt's method applied to the same data as we employed in the Brown's

Table 5.4   Holt's method: $\alpha = 0.3$, $\gamma = 0.1$

Period	Data	Smoothed data	Smoothed trend	Forecast $(m=1)$	Error
1	78.2	78.20	0.40		
2	78.6	78.60	0.40		
3	80.2	79.36	0.44	79.00	−1.20
4	81.6	80.34	0.49	79.80	−1.80
5	77.6	79.86	0.39	80.83	3.23
6	84.1	81.41	0.51	80.25	−3.85
7	78.5	80.89	0.41	81.92	3.42
8	83.7	82.02	0.48	81.30	−2.40
9	85.6	83.43	0.57	82.50	−3.10
10	85.2	84.36	0.61	84.00	−1.20
11	84.5	84.83	0.59	84.97	0.47
12	80.4	83.91	0.44	85.42	5.02
13	82.5	83.80	0.39	84.36	1.86
14	81.8	83.47	0.32	84.19	2.39
15	86.0	84.45	0.38	83.79	−2.21
16	82.4	84.10	0.31	84.83	2.43
17	83.4	84.11	0.28	84.41	1.01
18	85.9	84.84	0.32	84.39	−1.51
19	85.3	85.21	0.33	85.16	−0.14
20	84.1	85.10	0.29	85.53	1.43
21	88.1	86.20	0.37	85.39	−2.71
22	84.0	85.80	0.29	86.57	2.57
23	84.9	85.73	0.25	86.09	1.19
24	86.5	86.14	0.27	85.98	−0.52
25				86.41	
26				86.68	
27				86.95	
28				87.22	
29				87.49	
30				87.75	
31				88.02	
32				88.29	
33				88.56	
34				88.83	
35				89.10	
36				89.37	

Mean absolute error	1.78
Mean absolute percentage error	2.12
Mean square error	4.52
Mean error	0.67
(all for time periods 10−24)	

method example. For $t = 1$ we can initialize $S_1 = y_1 = 78.2$. However, we also need to supply a starting value for b_1. Since this is a first estimate of the slope of the line it seems sensible to use $y_2 - y_1$ as the starting value. Thus we have

$$b_1 = y_2 - y_1 = 78.6 - 78.2 = 0.4$$

In this case our starting value is sensible. Sometimes, however, we may find that y_2 is much less than y_1. If this happens our initial estimate of b_1 will be large and negative. It is normal to use a low value of γ to smooth the trend term (we have used 0.1 in this example). A low value of γ, together with a large and negative starting value for b_1, means that it will be a considerable number of data periods before the estimate of b_t will be positive (as one might expect). If this happens it is sensible to substitute a more reasonable value of b_1 so that the system does not take an inordinately long time to settle down. This problem of sensitivity to starting values requires careful vigilance.

For $t = 2$

$$\begin{aligned} S_2 &= 0.3 \times 78.6 + 0.7 \times (78.2 + 0.4) \\ &= 78.6 \end{aligned}$$

using equation (5.8), and

$$\begin{aligned} b_2 &= 0.1 \times (78.6 - 78.2) + 0.9 \times 0.4 \\ &= 0.4 \end{aligned}$$

using equation (5.9).

For $t = 3$

$$\begin{aligned} \hat{y}_3 &= 78.6 + 0.4 \\ &= 79.0 \end{aligned}$$

using equation (5.10).

This process continues until we reach the end of the data. Thereafter we produce m-step-ahead forecasts using equation (5.10) as follows:

$$\begin{aligned} \hat{y}_{25} &= 86.14 + 0.27 = 86.41 \\ \hat{y}_{26} &= 86.14 + 2 \times 0.27 = 86.68 \end{aligned}$$

and so on.

Parameter values of α between 0.1 and 0.3, and γ around 0.1, are commonly used for Holt's method.

5.3.3 Selection of optimal parameters

In the exponential smoothing example we explored different parameter values in order to provide an optimal forecasting procedure for future data points. We would normally do the same when carrying out Brown's or Holt's method. Essentially, we would calculate the MSE over all the data excluding the first few points (to allow the method to settle down) and then choose the value(s) of the parameter(s) which minimize this MSE. An important point needs to be addressed. We are minimizing the MSE for one-step-ahead forecasts and then using the optimal parameter(s) to provide m-step-ahead forecasts. The parameter which works best in producing one-step-ahead forecasts will not necessarily do best for longer time horizons. However, there is little we can do about this apart from noting the difficulty and being prepared for the consequences. If after a period of operating the forecasting procedure the forecasts appear to be poor, then we can explore what would have happened if we had used other values of the parameter(s) — this may lead to preferable values of the parameters by what is essentially an out-of-sample method.

5.3.4 Holt—Winters' method

Holt—Winters' method is an extension of Holt's method. In this case we append a third smoothing equation to allow for seasonality in the original data series. The equations for monthly data are as follows:

$$S_t = \alpha \frac{y_t}{I_{t-12}} + (1-\alpha)(S_{t-1} + b_{t-1}) \qquad (5.11)$$

$$b_t = \gamma(S_t - S_{t-1}) + (1-\gamma)b_{t-1} \qquad (5.12)$$

$$I_t = \beta \frac{y_t}{S_t} - (1-\beta)I_{t-12} \qquad (5.13)$$

$$\hat{y}_{t+m} = (S_t + mb_t)I_{t+m} \qquad (5.14)$$

These four equations estimate the level, trend, seasonality and forecast respectively. Since the seasonality is estimated by exponential smoothing it allows for changing seasonality as time proceeds (for instance, December could be seeing a steadily lower percentage of the total sales as the years go by). This sort of seasonality can also be captured by the X-11 procedure (see Chapter 20) but not by the standard moving average method which assumes constant seasonal factors for each month or quarter. Most practitioners find it easier to adjust data seasonally by X-11 and then to submit the seasonally adjusted data to Holt's method rather than to use Holt—Winters' method on the original data. Seasonally adjusted data are usually required for other purposes anyway, and the adjustment procedure within Holt—Winters' method is inferior to the X-11 procedure and suffers from the need to provide stable starting conditions (see Section 5.3.2).

Summary

Short-term forecasts assume either that the data set is stationary or that it has a trend. If it is stationary then we can use the naive method, although this suffers from forecasts which are not smooth. However, it is a good bench-mark against which to assess other methods. A simple moving average will provide smoother forecasts, but will also weight the most recent data as heavily as less recent data. This objection is circumvented by means of single exponential smoothing, which utilizes a parameter to regulate how rapidly the moving average weights decay away.

Non-stationary series are more common in sales and market data. Brown's method is a single-parameter method which uses double exponential smoothing to allow for a trend in the data. The slope of the line is continually updated by the exponential smoothing procedure. Holt's method also uses exponential smoothing as a basis, but it employs two parameters, one to estimate the level of the series and one to model the slope of the line. Both Brown's and Holt's methods suffer from difficulties in providing sensible starting values, but despite this they work very efficiently. In-sample fitting can be employed in either case to estimate the optimal parameters for a particular data set. Holt–Winters' method is similar to Holt's method, except that it adds a third parameter to allow for changing seasonality. In practice, practitioners tend to use Holt's method on seasonally adjusted data rather than Holt–Winters' method on raw data.

Short-term forecasting 2
Autoregressive models

6.1 Introduction

Chapter 5 dealt with short-term forecasting from the point of view of exponential smoothing — an *ad hoc* procedure which makes few assumptions about the data, but which works very well in practice. Chapter 6 considers the class of models known as *autoregressive* (AR) models in which assumptions are made about how one data point relates to previous data values. As with exponential smoothing models, AR models can deal with data sets which are stationary or have a trend. Section 6.4 then briefly explains how AR models can be extended into what is known as the Box—Jenkins form.

6.2 Autocorrelation

Very often the value of a data point in a time series depends heavily on the value of the previous point. For example, it is well known that, in the short term at least, the best forecast of tomorrow's stock exchange index is equal to today's index. This is known as a *random walk*. In other cases the relationship between today's value and tomorrow's value may be less strong, but still significant — this is often the case with daily sales data. In order to measure the strength of the relationship between two adjacent points we need to calculate the correlation between them. Such a correlation of a series with the same series lagged by one period is known as an *autocorrelation with lag 1*. The formula for this is as follows:

$$r_1 = \frac{\sum_{t=2}^{n} (y_t - \bar{y})(y_{t-1} - \bar{y})}{\sum_{t=1}^{n} (y_t - \bar{y})^2} \tag{6.1}$$

In a similar way we can explore the possibility of significant relationships between points j time periods apart. Here we need to calculate the autocorrelation coefficient with lag j. This is given by the following general expression:

$$r_j = \frac{\sum\limits_{t=j+1}^{n} (y_t - \bar{y})(y_{t-j} - \bar{y})}{\sum\limits_{t=1}^{n} (y_t - \bar{y})^2} \tag{6.2}$$

assuming that n is reasonably large.

For example, monthly sales data for a rapidly growing high-tech application are given in Table 6.1. Using equations (6.1) and (6.2) for the autocorrelation coefficients we obtain the following:

$$r_1 = \frac{\sum\limits_{t=2}^{12} (y_t - \bar{y})(y_{t-1} - \bar{y})}{\sum\limits_{t=1}^{12} (y_t - \bar{y})^2} = 0.57$$

$$r_2 = \frac{\sum\limits_{t=3}^{12} (y_t - \bar{y})(y_{t-2} - \bar{y})}{\sum\limits_{t=1}^{12} (y_t - \bar{y})^2} = 0.46$$

The question now is whether these coefficients are significant and if so how can we incorporate the information into an AR model.

If we plot the autocorrelation coefficients against their lags then we obtain what is known as a *correlogram*. The correlogram for the above example is shown in Figure 6.1. If r_j is close to $+1$ or -1 then we know that there may be a relationship between y_t and y_{t-j} which will necessitate an AR model.

Autocorrelations of random data have a standard deviation of approximately $1/\sqrt{n}$.

Table 6.1 Monthly sales of a rapidly growing product

Time	y_t	y_{t-1}	y_{t-2}
1	246		
2	260	246	
3	250	260	246
4	276	250	260
5	290	276	250
6	284	290	276
7	282	284	290
8	292	282	284
9	294	292	282
10	314	294	292
11	300	314	294
12	320	300	314

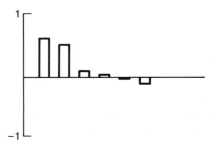

Figure 6.1 Example correlogram

Therefore, to test the significance of any of the autocorrelation coefficients we can apply confidence limits of $\pm t/\sqrt{n}$, where t follows a student's t-distribution. Normally we approximate to 95 per cent confidence limits by using $\pm 2/\sqrt{n}$. It must be stressed that this is only an approximation which is not valid for small data sets (such as we have in the example). Any reputable forecasting package will, however, use the exact confidence limits. For the sake of simplicity, though, we will continue to use the approximation for this example. It is normal to plot a correlogram with confidence limits superimposed, as shown, for our example, in Figure 6.2.

It is clear from Figure 6.2 that none of the autocorrelations is significant, due largely to the small sample size. We can therefore reject the need to build an AR model in this particular case. On the other hand, had we obtained the same autocorrelations using a sample of size 50 then the confidence limits would have been much tighter (equal to ± 0.28) and the first two autocorrelations would have been significant, so that we would have needed to build an AR model.

Before we consider how to identify AR models, however, it is necessary to understand the role of partial autocorrelation coefficients. If the autocorrelation coefficient with lag 1 is high, then it is quite likely that the autocorrelation coefficient with lag 2 will also be high. This is because today's value is strongly affected by yesterday's value, and also yesterday's value is strongly affected by the previous day's value. Therefore, there is likely to be quite a strong relationship between the values for today and two days ago, which

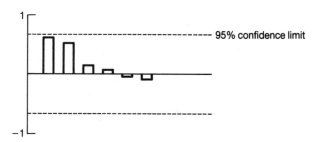

Figure 6.2 Example correlogram with confidence limits

will lead to a fairly high autocorrelation with lag 2. This high autocorrelation does not imply that we need to build a model incorporating both lags 1 and 2, however.

We clearly have a problem in identifying from the correlogram when we need to use higher-order lags in an AR model — significant autocorrelations do not imply causality. For this reason we need to employ the *partial autocorrelation coefficient*. This tells us what the autocorrelation coefficients would have been after removing the effects of all smaller lags. For instance, the partial autocorrelation coefficient with lag 2 eliminates the effect of the autocorrelation coefficient with lag 1, the autocorrelation coefficient with lag 3 eliminates the effects of lags 1 and 2, and so on. The partial autocorrelation function is analytically complicated, but is available on all good forecasting packages. Its confidence limits are $\pm t/\sqrt{n}$, where once again t has a student's t-distribution: commonly 95 per cent confidence limits of $\pm 2/\sqrt{n}$ are used. We therefore have two diagnostic tools to help us analyze potential AR models — the autocorrelation function (ACF) and the partial autocorrelation function (PACF).

6.3 Autoregressive models

The general AR model is given by the following expression:

$$y_t = a + b_1 y_{t-1} + b_2 y_{t-2} + \ldots + b_k y_{t-k} + \epsilon_t$$

where ϵ_t is distributed normally. This is a stationary model, and therefore a non-stationary series will need to be detrended by differencing or some other method before the AR model can be fitted. One problem attached to the fitting of AR models is that the terms on the right-hand side of the equation are not independent. If we use ordinary least squares to estimate the parameters then the values of the bs will be underestimated. Fortunately, this becomes less of a problem for large data series, so it is important to use large data sets when building AR models.

If it is suspected that an AR model will fit the data then the ACF will test stationarity and the PACF will indicate the lagged variables required. If the ACF decays to a value greater than zero, then the series is non-stationary and requires detrending (see Figure 6.3). If the ACF decays to zero then the series is stationary and suitable for modelling as an AR process (see Figure 6.4). If the ACF does not decay smoothly then we need to consider moving average terms, and the model will be more complicated than a pure AR process — see Section 6.4 on Box—Jenkins models.

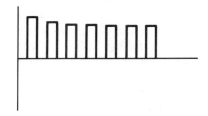

Figure 6.3 ACF indicating non-stationarity

Figure 6.4   ACF indicating stationarity

The PACF indicates the lags required in an AR model. Some words of warning are necessary here. We should not blindly fit all significant lags in the PACF. As a general rule the more terms the model possesses the more inaccurate the forecasts are likely to be (although the fit to the historic data may well be very good). We therefore try to minimize the number of terms in our model — this is known as the principle of *parsimony*. Generally we will try out simple models first. For example, suppose our PACF appeared to indicate an AR model with two terms (one of lag 1 and one, just significant, of lag 4). We would probably try an AR model with just the one term (lag 1) first since the other term was only just significant and was, in any case, a relatively high-order lag. In order to test the adequacy of the simpler model we would calculate the ACF and PACF of the residuals left after fitting the model — if no lags were significant, then we could assume that the simple model was doing an adequate job and that no further terms were necessary.

There is another reason for discarding lags which are just significant on the PACF. We are looking at a number of lags in a correlogram and testing each one of them for significance. The more lags we test the more likely it is that we will find a significant lag. For example, if we plot 20 lags then we have an even chance of achieving 95 per cent significance with at least one of the lags even if the series does not have any autoregressive properties. Another reason for ignoring a significant lag would be if we were talking about lag 12 (for monthly data). A significant PACF at lag 12 almost certainly indicates seasonality in the data series which should be taken out before resubmitting the adjusted data to ACF and PACF analysis.

For example, Figure 6.5 shows monthly values of the *Financial Times* All-Share Index for UK stocks running from the beginning of 1970 to the end of 1978. We wish to produce a one-month-ahead forecast for this series. We therefore consider an AR model as each data point may well depend heavily on the previous points. To test this assertion, we need to examine the ACF and the PACF of the series. These are shown in Figures 6.6 and 6.7, respectively. The ACF appears to be decaying slowly and therefore supports the hypothesis of short-term stationarity. The PACF shows a very high correlation at lag 1 followed by much smaller correlations for lags 2, 3, ... We will therefore consider the AR model of order 1 — usually written AR(1) — first, partly because the partial autocorrelation with lag 2 is only just significant and partly because it shows a negative coefficient which is hard to support from a practical point of view. In addition, it is preferable to use simpler models rather than complex ones.

Figure 6.8 shows the output from the statistical package STATGRAPHICS in estimating

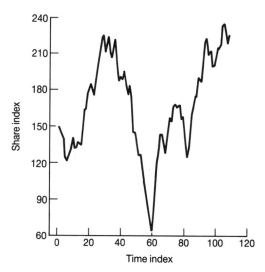

Figure 6.5 Monthly values of the FT All-Share Index, 1970–8

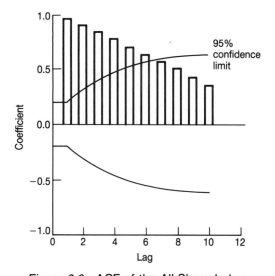

Figure 6.6 ACF of the All-Share Index

the model. Notice that the estimation procedure is iterative and that the significance of the AR term is very high. The fitted model is therefore

$$\hat{y}_t = 1.90 + 0.9875y_{t-1}$$

This is very close to the classical 'random walk' model which is typical of short-term stock-market behaviour. The perfect random walk would be given by

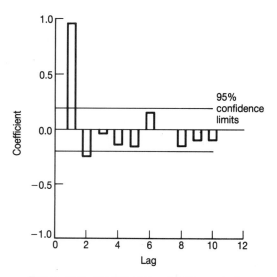

Figure 6.7   PACF of the All-Share Index

Estimation begins ....
Initial: RSS = 10121.4   b = 0.960427 166.504
Iteration 1: RSS = 9911.63   b = 0.973211 158.891
Iteration 2: RSS = 9850.73   b = 0.981966 154.255
Iteration 3: RSS = 9840.66   b = 0.986074 152.276
Final: RSS = 9839.63   .... stopped on criterion 2

Summary of Fitted Model for: −144 DROP FT02.var1

Parameter	Estimate	Stnd. error	T-value	P-value
AR(1)	0.98750	0.02231	44.27130	0.00000
MEAN	151.64055	9.54664	15.88418	0.00000
CONSTANT	1.89567			

Figure 6.8   STATGRAPHICS output, AR(1) model

$\hat{y}_t = y_{t-1}$

Using the fitted model we can produce short-term forecasts as follows. Suppose that our latest data point y_t is 200. Then our forecast for y_{t+1} is

$$y_{t+1} = 1.90 + 0.9875 \times 200$$
$$= 1.90 + 197.5$$
$$= 199.4$$

Similarly, a two-month-ahead forecast would be

$$y_{t+2} = 1.90 + 0.9875 \times \hat{y}_{t+1}$$
$$= 1.90 + 0.9875 \times 199.4$$
$$= 198.8$$

It is important not to get carried away and extend this process too far into the future. As we shall see, other methods become more appropriate for medium- and long-term forecasting — in the case of stock-market indices some correlation is likely with the trade cycle which we shall consider in the next chapter. A more pragmatic reason for restricting the length of the forecast is, however, that the theoretical confidence limits rapidly become very wide.

We have accepted the results of this AR(1) model here without further investigation. In practice, we would carry out diagnostic checks to ensure the adequacy of the fit. In common with the Box—Jenkins procedure (see Section 6.4), these diagnostic procedures would include an appraisal of the ACF and the PACF of the residuals left after fitting the model. In this particular case, the ACF and PACF imply that there is no further factor which is likely to provide significant additional power in the forecasting equation, so the AR(1) model is sufficient for our purposes.

6.4 Box—Jenkins models

Box and Jenkins (1976) extended the AR models we have considered in this chapter to allow for the possibility that the ACF may well not display a decaying curve which would indicate a straight AR model. A great deal of statistical analysis has been carried out on Box—Jenkins methods, and there is little doubt that these have particularly elegant statistical properties. They also perform well for short-term forecasting. However, they also require an expert to run them because they are far from automatic models. This is because they depend on a visual assessment of ACF and PACF. In addition, they are complex to calculate and therefore prohibitively expensive and time-consuming for the most common industrial short-term forecasting problems. These tend to involve the production process where many grade ranges need to be forecast at frequent intervals. This combination of cost, time and expertise requirements has led to a very limited use of the method in industry and commerce. Furthermore, Makridakis *et al.* (1982) found very little difference between the performance of the simpler, cheaper and automatic Holt's method and the Box—Jenkins model. For these reasons we will examine the basics of the method only. The interested reader has a choice of many texts which explore the Box—Jenkins method at considerable length (see, for example, O'Donovan 1983).

The general class of AR models is given by the expression

$$y_t = a + b_1 y_{t-1} + b_2 y_{t-2} + \ldots + b_k y_{t-k}$$

where the parameters a and b_i are to be estimated.

In addition, the general class of moving average (MA) models is given by the equation

$$y_t = a + b_1 e_{t-1} + b_2 e_{t-2} + \ldots + b_k e_{t-k}$$

where the parameters a and b_i are again to be estimated and the quantities e_i are the errors or residuals of the model at various time periods.

It is possible to combine AR and MA models to form what are known as *ARMA* models. Furthermore, if we allow for the possibililty of differencing the data to achieve stationarity,

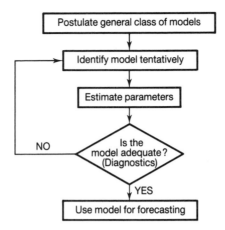

Figure 6.9   The iterative Box—Jenkins technique

then the model becomes an *integrated* model and is known as an *ARIMA* model. This general class of models is also known as Box—Jenkins models.

The method of arriving at a suitable model to describe the data is an iterative one; the procedure is illustrated in Figure 6.9. We suppose that we are willing to postulate the general class of Box—Jenkins models and use the ACF and the PACF to identify tentatively a suitable model from the general class of models. Having identified a suitable model, we need to estimate its parameters. This is itself an iterative procedure which can be quite time-consuming. We now need to check whether the model is adequate. This is achieved by a number of diagnostic measures. Of key importance is a further ACF and PACF carried out on the residuals. If this shows further significant influences then the model must be rejected and we return to identify tentatively another model which we hope will meet the objections to the first model. This model is then estimated and diagnostics are produced. When we find a satisfactory model which creates satisfactory diagnostics, we can use that model for forecasting.

Unfortunately, satisfactory diagnostics do not imply that the best model has been fitted. It is possible to estimate a number of models which give satisfactory diagnostics — the first one we arrive at may not be the best. In practice, this problem is circumvented by using the principle of parsimony mentioned in Section 6.3. This has the backing of empirical studies which show that parsimonious models tend to forecast better than complicated models, although the complicated ones will usually fit the data better!

6.4.1   Model identification

The ACF and the PACF are used to identify the model to be examined. Theoretically, AR models are characterized by a gradually declining ACF, with a PACF which cuts off at the order of the AR model to be estimated. Similarly, MA models involve ACFs which

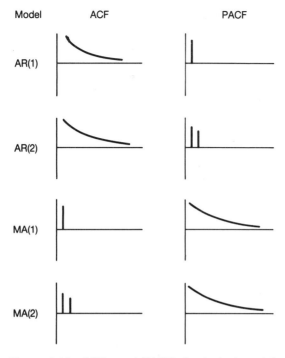

Figure 6.10   ACFs and PACFs for typical models

cut off at the order of the model to be fitted, whereas the PACF gradually declines. Mixed (ARIMA) models have some mixtures of these attributes. The theoretical ACFs and PACFs are shown in Figure 6.10.

In practice, the identification of a model is a matter of considerable expertise, as the ACF and/or PACF will tend to deviate markedly from theory, and interpretation can vary. These difficulties form the practical objection to the widespread use of Box–Jenkins methods in industry.

6.5 Summary

If a data point tends to depend on the value of previous data points, then an autoregressive (AR) model is indicated. The autocorrelation coefficient measures the correlation of a series with itself lagged by a certain number of time periods. The correlogram is a plot of the autocorrelation function (ACF) against lag. The partial autocorrelation function (PACF) measures the autocorrelation coefficients after allowing for smaller lags. The suitability and order of an AR model can be assessed by looking at the ACF and PACF: a decaying ACF and a cut-off in the PACF at lag j implies an AR model of order j.

Box—Jenkins (ARIMA) models extend the AR model to include the possibility of a moving average (MA) model or a mixed (ARMA) model. Differencing is allowed for in ARIMA models. The process of fitting an ARIMA model is iterative and involves examining the ACF and PACF of the data and the residuals. The identification of the ARIMA model to be fitted is often problematical and requires the attention of an expert. The whole process is lengthly and not suitable for typical short-term industrial forecasting, where many forecasts have to be processed in a short time using an automatic routine.

CHAPTER 7

Medium-term forecasting 1
The trade cycle

7.1 Introduction

Product sales rarely grow in a steady fashion. Although there may be an underlying trend in growth, there are likely to be deviations from that trend due to a number of factors. First, monthly or quarterly data will often show seasonal deviations due to the existence of traditionally strong or weak periods. A second cause of deviations from the underlying trend, which we shall discuss in this and succeeding chapters, is the existence of medium- and/or long-term cycles in the data. Although we can incorporate further factors such as discontinuities, it is difficult to model these. This is not to say that they are unpredictable, as we shall see in Chapter 12. It makes sense to disentangle the trend and cyclical effects — it is generally unsatisfactory to amalgamate both influences as the resultant trend/cycle has a growth rate which oscillates wildly. One case in which it is reasonable to amalgamate the trend and cycle is when our only aim is to extract seasonal factors — this is true for the X-11 seasonal adjustment routine described in Chapter 20.

The general medium- to long-term sales volume model can thus be thought of as

$$Y = T + C + S + E$$

where Y is sales volume, T trend, C cycle(s), S a seasonal factor and E error or residual. This procedure is known as *decomposition*.

7.2 The trade cycle

The aim of this chapter is to explore the nature of the most important cycle found in economic life, namely the *trade cycle*, or, as it has become known in the USA, the *business cycle*.

One of the earliest references to the trade cycle is to be found in the papers of Lord Overstone in the nineteenth century, where he described trade as passing through a number of phases in a cyclical fashion. These phases he described as stagnation, improvement, confidence, prosperity, excitement and convulsion. The cyclical nature of the economy has since been recognized, although economists have differed as to the prime causes of the cycle. At various stages the cycle has been promounced 'dead', but such pronouncements have always proved to be premature.

The postwar trade cycle in the UK can be seen in Figure 7.1, which shows the annual movement of the industrial production index (IPI). Figure 7.2 transforms the data in Figure 7.1 by calculating annual percentage changes in the IPI data. This shows how growth in the index rises and falls once every 4–5 years. In the 1960s the trough growth rate remained positive, but in the 1970s troughs became recessions (that is, they became negative for a period). Figure 7.3 shows the growth rate for manufacturing production (a subset of the total IPI figure). The cyclical nature of these data is even clearer than for the IPI as a whole. This gives us a clue as to the origin of the cycle: we will pursue this in our consideration of Forrester's model in Section 7.3.

This cycle can be seen in most of the developed economies in the world. The length of the cycle is roughly the same on average, but the phasing can vary slightly. For example, US production tends to lead European production by around 9 months. In other words,

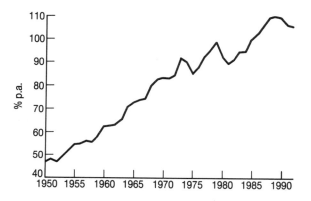

Figure 7.1   Industrial production index, UK (1985 = 100)

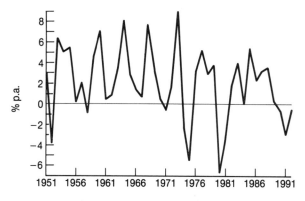

Figure 7.2   Rate of growth of industrial production, UK, 1951–92

the USA passes through its peaks and troughs about 9 months ahead of Europe. Sometimes extraneous shocks to the system increase the residuals around a perfect cyclical shape, but the cycle becomes clear again very soon afterwards. Often a shock to the system will increase or decrease the amplitude of the trade cycle rather than change its phasing or length. For example, the original oil shock when prices were raised in 1974 helped to deepen the 1975 recession and the fall in oil prices in the mid-1980s helped to decrease the amplitude of the 1986 downturn (see Figure 7.3).

It is important to understand the underlying causes behind the trade cycle in order to be able to counteract the swings as they occur. As we shall see, the causes are likely to remain with us whatever counter-cyclical policies the governments of the world decide to employ. We therefore need to assume that the cycles are going to continue, but we also need to work out ways of predicting the timing, predicting the amplitude, and providing suitable planning responses from a corporate point of view. The next few chapters indicate how we can approach these problems. Forecasting and planning for cyclical movements is not easy, but the problem is pervasive and so important to the average business that we cannot afford to ignore it.

7.3 A simulation approach

Why should a cycle occur if the various business forces at work are non-cyclical in nature? This has puzzled many a businessman, but the answer is to be found in the natural sciences, where cycles are quite commonplace. One of the mainsprings of cycles is the existence of a lag between a force and the response to that force. So we should look for suitable lags in the economic and business systems which make up the business world. One such lag is the delay between a change in the level of demand and the corporate response in terms of higher output. The business executive will typically fail to recognize the change in demand level immediately due to the existence of natural variability. For a month or two he/she may see the upturn in orders as being due to a one-off event and feel that it

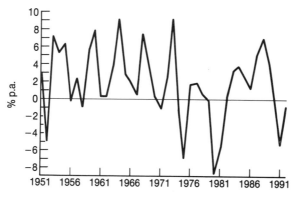

Figure 7.3 Rate of growth of manufacturing production, UK, 1951–92

could easily be reversed. He/she will be reluctant to sanction an increase in production until it is certain that the change in demand will endure. Once he/she has made the decision to raise production levels it will be some time before production has fully adjusted to the change in demand because extra stocks of raw materials need to be bought in, and probably extra human resources need to be recruited, and all this takes time. Figure 7.4 shows the response to a step-change in demand. Production slowly reacts and it is not until the point marked *A* that production is in line with the new level of demand.

In the meantime, stock levels have dipped as the difference between demand and production has to be satisfied from stock. At point *A* therefore, stocks are too low with respect to the previous low level of demand; stock to sales ratios are likely to be far too low for the new higher level of demand. Production will therefore be raised further in order to build up these stocks to a satisfactory level. By the point marked *B* stocks are back in line with demand. If demand really could be represented by a straight line then we would instantly cut our production back in line with demand and the cycle would cease. However, the lag between action and reaction continues to apply and it takes time for production to react to the satisfactory level of stocks. By the time production is back down to a satisfactory level, stocks have risen to a high level. No self-respecting accountant is likely to allow this, so production has to be reduced below the level of underlying demand in order to reduce stocks again. We therefore return to the initial position with production below demand, and the cycle can repeat itself.

Of course, none of this would happen if there were no random variation to cloud the business executive's judgement and if decisions could be enacted instantly. However, in the real world we *do* have variability in demand and we cannot enact decisions immediately, so we do tend to have cycles. It is also worth noting that once a cycle is started it tends to continue — in other words, we do not need a sequence of demand changes (or shocks to the system) to maintain a cycle. Indeed, as we shall see, we do not even need changes in the general level of demand!

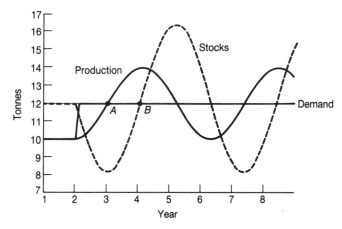

Figure 7.4 Effect of a step change in demand

In the 1970s, Forrester and his colleagues at the Massachusetts Institute of Technology developed what they called a *system dynamics* model of the US economy. This is essentially a simulation model in which many interactions in the economy are modelled in a deterministic fashion. For example, the consumer durables sector responds to changes in consumer demand by changing stock levels and recruiting labour after a lag. Such lags as these were estimated from US economic statistics and used in the model. Forrester was then in a position to examine the behaviour of key outputs such as sector production levels when inputs such as consumer demand were varied.

First, Forrester supplied the model with a steady demand level. Naturally the outputs of the model also remained steady. The presence of the lags in the system would undoubtedly create a cycle in the production output if we fed the model with a step change in demand — we have already seen why this should be so. However, Forrester made the important discovery that a step change in demand was unnecessary to stimulate a cycle in the resulting production. All that was needed was to feed the system with steady demand on which random variation was superimposed. It appears, therefore, that cycles are stimulated by random variation in demand alone, and of course the business world is not short of random variation in demand! Forrester discovered that cycles would be produced not only by step changes, but also by the natural conditions of the business world. In other words, we must expect cycles to exist whatever the business environment is doing.

Forrester manipulated the simulation model to test for the underlying causes of any cycles which may exist. In this chapter we consider only the main cycle — the trade cycle. We move on in Chapters 10 and 11 to look at two further cycles which Forrester modelled, and which have a substantial effect on company behaviour. Using the lags estimated from government statistics, a cycle of 4—5 years emerged when driven by random variation about a steady level of demand. When the lags between the consumer durables sector's seeing a new level of demand and its reacting by changing stock levels and human resource levels were constrained to zero, the cycle disappeared entirely. The lags were obviously the motivating factors as far as the trade cycle was concerned. These lags were also varied around their estimated values to test the sensitivity of the model, and it was found that although the cycle length changed as the lag length changed, the movement in the cycle length was far less than the movement in the lag. In other words, the cycle length was not overly sensitive to variations in the length of the lags.

Some industries are close to the consumer, and therefore follow the above analysis. Other industries are in the intermediate goods sector or the raw materials sector, and thus have a number of customers between them and the eventual consumer. For example, a petrochemical producer manufactures propylene. This is used by plastics manufacturers to make polypropylene. They, in turn, sell the polypropylene on to film manufacturers who turn it into polypropylene film. This can be used for packaging — for example, it is used in potato crisp bags. However, there is still a further stage to pass through — the film must be printed with the name of the product and other information. The printed film can now be used to bag crisps in the production process, and the crisps are finally taken to retail outlets to be sold to the public. The manufacturing chain is therefore a long one, and the effect of this is to magnify the amplitude of the cycle. For example, the crisp manufacturer sees only a random fluctuation in demand which transforms (as we have seen) into a cyclical crisp-production pattern. The printer who supplies the crisp manufacturer therefore sees demand as cyclical, since the crisp manufacturer is seeing cyclical production. The printer, therefore, is affected by cyclical demand and also the leads and lags which will amplify that cycle. The film manufacturer will see demand for film as being subject to greater swings than the printer's demand. This increase in the amplitude of the cycle as we move back along the production chain is known as the *pipeline effect*. It means that industries at the end of long chains can expect high-amplitude cycles — in the above example, we would expect the petrochemical industry to exhibit heavily cyclical production. It is vitally important for those industries which are at least partly removed from the final consumer to carry out effective cyclical forecasting and planning for their products.

There is one further implication arising from the nature of cyclical fluctuations. As we have seen, stocks play a large part in producing the trade cycle. Many econometric models of the national economy are very large — often involving several hundred equations. There are major statistical problems in retaining the stability of such a set of equations, especially as the normal statistical assumptions underlying such models are often violated. For this reason a residual effect is often controlled in order to force stability into the econometric model. It is very tempting to use stock-building in the economy as this residual effect. However, if we manipulate stock-building instead of allowing the model to estimate it, we may well distort the main motivating force in producing a cyclical pattern to production. This would indeed stabilize the forecast at the expense of removing the cycle. Forecasts from the main econometric models often exhibit very little in the way of medium-term cyclical movement — or, to put it another way, large-amplitude cycles are rarely forecast well by such models. It may well be that manipulating stock forecasts is to blame. Predicting marked cyclical upswings or downswings is very important to manufacturing businesses — such predictions cannot be made on the basis of econometric forecasts. In Section 7.5 we will discuss another way in which companies can anticipate rapid cyclical movements.

The extent to which the pipeline effect amplifies cyclical production movements is shown in Figure 7.5. This indicates the amplitude of the cycle for the sum of three bulk polymers

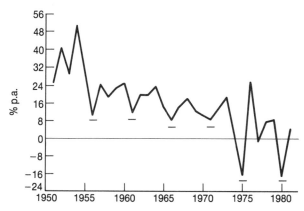

Figure 7.5 Growth of UK market for LDPE, PVC and PP, 1951–81

in the UK. For example, 1974 saw a 20 per cent increase in the market whereas 1975 rebounded with a 17 per cent fall. These figures are much more accentuated than the equivalent figures for industrial production in the same years. Figure 7.5 demonstrates the importance in the bulk polymer business of predicting not only the timing of the cycle but also the amplitude. There is a world of difference between recessionary *growth* of 8–10 per cent as seen in the four recessions between 1956 and 1971 and the 17 per cent *decline* seen in 1975 and 1980.

The international nature of the cycle is displayed in Figure 7.6, in which the similarities of the cyclical patterns in western Europe and the UK are readily apparent by comparison with Figure 7.5.

7.4 Consumer demand and the trade cycle

We have explored the importance of stocking and destocking to the trade cycle. Turning points in the cycle are usually mirrored by turning points in stockholding. However, there are other elements of final demand which are often examined to see whether there is any evidence of a turning point in industrial activity. The most common situation involves the monitoring of retail sales or consumers expenditure — typically commentators look for a turnaround in consumer demand to herald a turning point in the trade cycle. This can be an unrewarding exercise, as Figures 7.7 and 7.8 illustrate. These show the UK market for low density polyethylene (LDPE), polyvinyl chloride (PVC) and polypropylene (PP), and retail sales volume over a period which covers the two major recessions of 1975 and 1980. It is clear that retail sales fell during the downturn into 1975. However, while plastics output, in common with the rest of UK industrial output, recovered strongly in 1976, retail sales continued to decline until 1978. Anyone looking for a recovery in retail sales to signal the end of the recession would have been two years too late! Similarly, retail sales growth slackened but did not reverse in 1980 while a major recession was under way. Consumer demand is, therefore, unreliable in signalling cyclical changes.

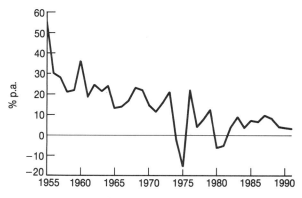

Figure 7.6 Growth of western European market for LDPE, PVC and PP, 1955–91

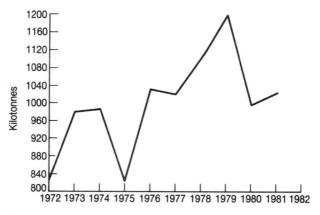

Figure 7.7   UK market for LDPE, PVC and PP, 1972–81

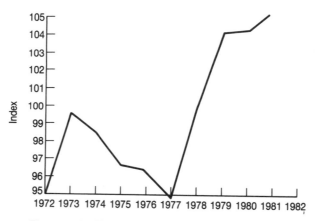

Figure 7.8   Retail sales volume, UK, 1972–81

7.5   A short-term predictor of the trade cycle

We have seen that stockholding is important in shaping the trade cycle, and that consumer demand is not. However, we really require a measure which *leads* the cycle in industrial output, so that we have time to make decisions when we can foresee a cyclical upturn or downturn ending. Such a short-term forecasting device is indicated in Figures 7.9 and 7.10. These graphs show short-term UK interest rates (the Bank Base Rate) and UK stockbuilding. The latter is inverted — that is, stockbuilding is shown by a negative change while stockshedding is indicated by a positive one. Interest rates move much more steadily than stockbuilding, but the main trends are clear. During the course of a trade cycle, interest rates often see more than one peak: in the 17 years of data in Figure 7.9 we can see two

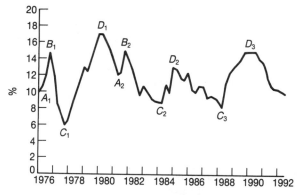

Figure 7.9 UK Bank Base Rate, 1976–92

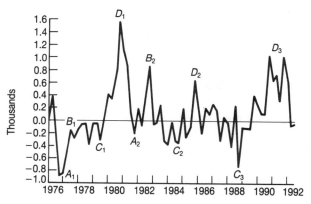

Figure 7.10 UK stockbuilding, 1976–92 (inverted)

peaks in interest rates during each of the first two cycles. The first cycle sees peaks at B_1 and D_1, whereas the equivalent points in the second cycle are at B_2 and D_2. Troughs can be seen at A_1, C_1, A_2 and C_2. The same system of lettering is shown on the stockbuilding graph (Figure 7.10). However, in the final cycle there are only two turning points, C_3 and D_3. A_3 and B_3 have, therefore, been omitted. By examining the relative positions of the letters on each of the two graphs, we can see that the peaks and troughs in interest rates always precede the peaks and troughs in stockbuilding. For example, the peak in interest rates in 1980, D_1, preceded the worst of the stocksshedding seen in 1981 (also D_1). There is some variation in the lead time, but on average it is around 9 months. In addition, a large swing in interest rates (for instance, C_1D_1) gives rise to a large swing in stockbuilding, and small swings tend to go together as well. We therefore have a useful short-term predictor of the timing and extent of trade-cycle swings.

For example, the extended swing in interest rates C_1D_1 forecast a severe downturn in stockbuilding approximately 9 months later, thus providing early warning of a marked downturn in industrial output. We shall extend this concept when we move on to the subject of leading indicators. Forecasting the timing of the trade cycle therefore divides into two complementary parts. First, we can approximate to the timing of the cycle by observing that the cycle normally lasts for around 5 years. This gives us a rough idea of cycle timing some years ahead. We can then home in more accurately nearer the time by using the 9-month lead of interest rates: using interest rates also indicates the likely amplitude of the forthcoming cyclical upswing or downswing.

In summary, interest rates lead stock changes, and stock changes drive the cycle in production. Therefore, interest rates will lead cyclical changes in production growth. It would be nice to think that the cycle could be eliminated by maintaining a steady level of interest rates. Unfortunately, the government is often forced into interest-rate changes. For example, the government will raise interest rates to defend a weak currency or to curb excessive growth in the money supply which might lead to high inflation. At other times it might lower interest rates in order to stimulate stagnant industrial production levels. The general pressure on interest rates is dictated by world-wide trends in interest rates, and it is difficult for a national government to maintain steady rates when the world-wide trend is strongly upward or downward.

7.6 The trade-cycle clock

Although industrial production or gross domestic product (GDP) is normally used to define the timing of the trade cycle, other economic indicators also describe cycles, either leading or lagging production. For example, share prices tend to lead production by several months. Thus share prices will tend to reach a minimum *before* the trough of industrial production. Similarly, shares will peak before the peak of production. On the other hand, it is usually some time *after* the trough in industrial production before unemployment peaks, and it is a considerable time after peak production before we reach the lowest level of unemployment. Indeed, unemployment is an example of a non-sinusoidal cycle — it rises very rapidly and falls over a longer period very slowly. We shall refer further to non-sinusoidal cycles in Chapter 9.

We can visually represent the changing 'seasons' of the trade cycle by means of a *trade-cycle clock* (see Figure 7.11). We describe the cycle as one revolution of the clock. We can start at 6 o'clock (where we have minimum industrial production), and work our way clockwise to 12 o'clock (maximum industrial production) and onwards back to minimum industrial production again. In the course of this revolution of the clock face we pass peaks and troughs of other economic variables such as unemployment, inflation, interest rates and share prices. Other variables could easily be added to the diagram once their lead or lag had been estimated with respect to industrial production. Variables whose cycles take the same time to rise as they do to fall (on average) will see their maxima and minima opposite one another on the clock — for example, share prices. On the other hand, non-sinusoidal cycles such as unemployment will not have maxima and minima opposite one another. For the purposes of Figure 7.11 we have only displayed the main maximum and

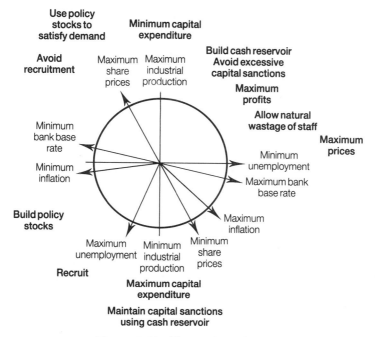

Figure 7.11 The trade-cycle clock

minimum on interest rates despite our analysis earlier which pointed to two peaks and troughs per cycle for this variable.

We can also place on the clock actions which a company should carry out to make the most of the properties of the cycle. These actions are marked in **bold** type around the outside of the maxima and minima of the economic variables. These actions are called *counter-cyclical*. In many cases they are contrary to the actions that human nature would dictate for that stage of the trade cycle. For example, when production is at its highest, there may well be pressure on plant, leading to a danger of loss of sales because either the plant is working flat out or because human resources are insufficient. Many works managers will be exhorting their boards of directors for more plant and more human resources on the basis that the extra profit that would be made would more than cover the cost of extra resources. However, this is a very short-term view and ignores the likelihood that as the production cycle goes into reverse, these extra resources will become redundant. It is therefore the time to minimize capital expenditure and to avoid employing extra manpower. This is a difficult strategy to follow since peak production will produce good profits and cash, and it is natural for boards to want to be optimistic and underpin further growth by spending the cash which peak production is providing. If cash is spent on capital plant, however, it may well be that the lag between agreeing the expenditure and seeing the plant working efficiently is 2−3 years. The plant therefore comes on stream just at the moment when it is least needed (at the bottom of the production cycle). The extra depreciation and fixed costs will lead to pressure on profits just when there is already substantial profit pressure due to low production.

The counter-cyclical strategy would be to avoid excessive capital sanctions at the peak of the production cycle and to save the cash in the form of a cash reservoir. This reservoir could be used for capital sanctions at the trough of the cycle because high capital sanctions at a trough will not be justified by the low level of cash generated by the business at this stage. However, the high level of plant sanctioned at the trough will become fully operational near the peak of the cycle when it will be most needed. As Figure 7.11 indicates, product prices will tend to reach a maximum some months after the peak in production (see also Chapter 17 on price forecasting). Profits will therefore reach a maximum somewhere between the maxima of production and prices. At this point it is useful to allow natural wastage of staff so that human resources can be reduced as cheaply as possible as the trough approaches. Allowing the number of workers employed to remain high as profits start to fall on the basis that the fall is only temporary is likely to lead to expensive enforced redundancies. Similarly, the time to recruit is when unemployment is at a maximum some time after the trough in production. This allows recruitment in the most receptive conditions and allows time for training before the next cyclical peak occurs. As the cycle moves upwards it is sensible to build policy stocks — these can be used to satisfy demand when production is at a peak and the plant may not be fully capable of coping with sudden monthly blips in demand.

Counter-cyclical planning therefore allows the efficient use of resources while looking beyond the short-term pressures of today to the cyclical movements several months ahead. Natural human optimism at times of peak cyclical activity is a pressure against sensible planning of this type, as is the pressure to cut costs at the trough of the cycle. The benefits of taking the longer-term view can be considerable, though, as case studies in this book will testify. Some companies adopt a sort of semi-counter-cyclical stance, and try to maintain capital sanctions throughout the cycle at a constant level. This is useful but not optimal.

Counter-cyclical decision-making is necessarily a function of the board of directors advised by its planning operation. This ensures that central decisions are taken which are away from the short-term pressures of a works environment. Since this sort of planning flies in the face of human nature, it does not evolve overnight, but tends to start in a small way before expanding in scope as the track record of the planners concerned is validated. This does not argue against the need for careful monitoring, however — the decisions taken need to be tracked and amended if necessary. Although the monitoring and prediction of the course of the trade cycle should give usable results (see Chapter 8) there remains the possibility of a peak occurring some months behind schedule or of a cyclical pickup being very sluggish. Such events can cause some fine tuning to be necessary to the counter-cyclical plans.

A major feature of this type of planning is that decisions, and implementation of those decisions, need to take place *before* the relevant cyclical event takes place. For example, if stocks in a heavily cyclical business are not minimized before a bout of destocking starts, then it may be impossible to reduce stocks as the downturn unfolds as many customers will cease ordering altogether. It is also important to distinguish between strategy and tactics. Tactics are short-term plans and are usually product-based. Strategy is longer-term and company-based. Strategic moves such as counter-cyclical planning need to take precedence over tactical moves in the marketplace.

This sort of planning is particularly valuable to companies which see marked cyclical movements in sales. These companies are to be found mainly in the manufacturing sector, and pipeline-sensitive industries will find marked benefits. The construction sectors would also benefit due to the influence of interest rates and the marked cyclical swings which it encounters. The service sector and the public sector are less affected by the cycle, and, therefore, would be less likely to use counter-cyclical planning. However, even these sectors are subject to cyclical influences to some extent, as economic pressures impact on such variables as consumer expenditure and the public sector borrowing requirement.

CHAPTER 8

Medium-term forecasting 2
Forecasting cyclical series

8.1 Introduction

Many business data series are strongly cyclical. Unfortunately, most forecasting techniques are relatively strong at predicting trends, but weaker at anticipating cyclical movements. This chapter looks at two methods of predicting the cyclical component of a data series: the first method is a short-term tool which operates up to 12 months ahead; the second method provides a framework for forecasting the cycle a matter of years in advance.

8.2 Leading indicators

Leading indicators aim to anticipate turning points in cyclical series. In order to do this we construct a time series which displays cyclical maxima and minima some months ahead of the data series we want to forecast. When this series, called the *leading indicator*, shows a peak or trough then we can expect the data series we want to forecast to show a peak or trough some months later. Leading indicators forecast the timing of turning points and not the magnitude of the upswing or downswing. They are therefore useful for *event-timing* forecasts.

In Chapter 7 we saw that movements in interest rates lead stockbuilding in the economy by some 9 months on average. Stockbuilding is an important factor in describing the cyclical movement in industrial production. We could, therefore, say that the rate of interest is a leading indicator for industrial production. Usually, however, we do not rely on a single time series as our leading indicator. Instead, we find a number of time series which have the properties of leading indicators, and form a weighted average of these to produce our final leading indicator. This guards against the possibility that one of the components may fail to give a clear signal at a given turning point. Our leading indicator is therefore formed as the sum of a number of economic factors and would be expected to perform as shown in Figure 8.1. In practice, as in Figure 8.1, a moving average of the sales series would be plotted in order to display a smoother graph and clarify the position of the peaks and troughs. The moving average used could well be the Henderson moving average output from the X-11 seasonal adjustment package (see Chapter 20).

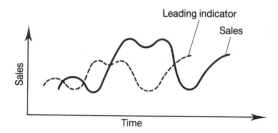

Figure 8.1 Sales volume and a leading indicator

Leading indicators are frequently used by governments in order to anticipate turning points in industrial production. For example, in the UK the Central Statistical Office issues two leading indicators: a longer-leading indicator and a shorter-leading indicator. The longer-leading indicator is the more frequently quoted: it has a lead time of around 12 months and consists of five factors:

1. share prices;
2. interest rates;
3. net acquisition of financial assets;
4. total number of dwellings started;
5. CBI quarterly survey — change in optimism.

Some of these factors are available immediately, but for others there is a lag before publication. The indicator is issued monthly using the latest available information for each series.

The leading indicator was constructed by examining a number of candidate components, and testing for their suitability. Factors were chosen by scoring highly on the following points:

1. economic significance;
2. statistical adequacy;
3. historical conformity with business cycles;
4. cyclical timing record as leaders;
5. smoothness;
6. promptness of publication.

Thus, for example, we would not consider sunspot cycles as a candidate as they have no economic significance. We would not consider a series which is frequently and/or heavily revised: such a series would not be 'statistically adequate'. We do look for a consistent pattern of rises and falls in line with the business cycle as displayed in industrial production, and we would require a consistent lead in the indicator components. Some data series are much smoother than others and turning points are therefore quickly isolated, and it is clearly of little use to have an indicator with a lead of 12 months if it is only published a year after the event!

In assessing the cyclical timing record of candidate components of a leading indicator we need to define the exact meaning of a peak or trough. Normally a peak is indicated if a certain number of successive months following the peak (usually 3 months) give values below the prospective peak. We need to monitor the number of times a component correctly forecasts a turning point and balance this against the number of times it identifies a peak or trough which never materializes. In addition, we need to assess the length of the lead — is the lead consistent or does it change systematically? In the latter case it may be of little use as a leading indicator component.

Leading indicators are used by manufacturing companies in two ways. If the timing of the sales cycle lines up closely with the timing of the industrial production cycle, then we can sensibly use the CSO longer-leading indicator to forecast cyclical changes in our sales pattern. However, it can be even more sensible to add other components which score highly for economic significance (that is, are closely allied to end-uses for the company's products). For example, in the 1970s ICI's Plastics Division developed a leading indicator which consisted of the CSO longer-leading indicator together with new car registrations, since new car registrations proved to be a good leading component and the motor car sector was an important end-use for the Division.

Of course, the CSO leading indicator would only be useful to predict peaks and troughs of UK sales. In the case of ICI's Plastics Division it was recognized that important sales were made in Europe, and particularly in West Germany. Because of this a leading indicator for the Division's West German sales was developed and used in parallel with the UK leading indicator.

8.3 Peak-to-peak forecasting

Leading indicators give a relatively short-term prediction of turning points in the economy or in a company's sales volume. However, we also need to be able to forecast sales series with cyclical tendencies in the rather longer term. We already have a rough and ready tool for predicting the timing of the cycle — the trade-cycle clock (Section 7.6). We also need to be able to predict the amplitude of the cycle. In many companies planners need to forecast sales on the basis of a medium-term forecast of industrial production. The peak-to-peak method allows them to do this in a consistent manner: it allows consistent forecasts to be made of a number of products on the basis of the same industrial production predictions.

The peak-to-peak method derives from unpublished work carried out in the UK Central Statistical Office. It splits the sales series into trend and cycle components, finds a link between the sales cycle and the industrial production cycle, and then projects sales using cyclical information derived from the industrial production forecast. The method is as follows:

1. Smooth the sales series by taking the seasonally adjusted data and applying a suitable moving average — as before, we can use the output of the X-11 package for this. Plot the series.
2. Identify the cyclical peaks and troughs. Join successive peaks and successive troughs together with straight lines.

3. Drop perpendiculars from each peak and raise perpendiculars from each trough. Join together the halfway points of each perpendicular with straight lines. This gives the trend of the data series. This trend stops at the peak or trough before last, since there is no peak-to-peak or trough-to-trough line beyond this point. We can extend the trend to the end of the data by drawing in a final peak-to-peak line (or trough-to-trough line as in Figure 8.2) which is parallel to the last straight line. For example, in Figure 8.2 we draw line *CD* parallel to line *AB*. This enables us to drop another perpendicular from point *B*, and calculate another midpoint (*E*), which allows us to extend the trend to point *E*. It is normal then to extend the trend further into the future to point *F* by continuing the last portion of the trend line in the same direction.

This constructs a trend for the whole length of the data in the form of a succession of straight lines. We now need to calculate the cycle around this trend, and to relate this cycle with the cycle for the industrial production index (IPI). We therefore continue our method as follows.

4. Calculate the percentage deviation of the sales line from the trend.
5. Construct a peak-to-peak diagram for the IPI.
6. Calculate the percentage deviation of the IPI line from its trend.
7. Plot a graph showing the percentage deviation of sales from its trend compared with the percentage deviation of IPI from its trend. This is shown in Figure 8.3.

For many products the timing of the peaks and troughs for the two series will line up

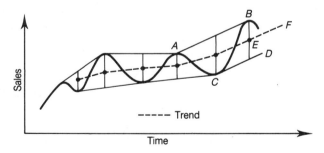

Figure 8.2   Construction of peak-to-peak diagram

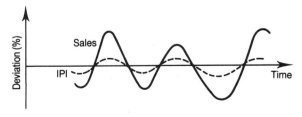

Figure 8.3   Deviations from trend

(on average), thereby showing that the product sales neither lead nor lag the economy as a whole. If a significant lead or lag is apparent then the following analysis needs to be modified to allow for the lead/lag. The next step allows us to forecast the amplitude of the sales cycle given the amplitude of the IPI cycle.

8. Calculate the multiplier between the amplitude of the sales cycle and the amplitude of the IPI cycle. This can be done exactly by regressing the sales deviation on the IPI deviation, thereby giving a multiplier b in the form

    Sales deviation (%) $= b \times$ IPI deviation (%)

    More commonly, we can calculate the deviations at each peak and trough for sales and IPI and estimate the average multiplier over all peaks and troughs. Although this latter method is less elegant, it is often used since
    (i) it simplifies the calculation;
    (ii) it concentrates on the peaks and troughs and not the points in between; and
    (iii) an exact estimate of b is unnecessary since the forecast of sales will depend on the forecast amplitude of the IPI cycle, which is undoubtedly subject to a fair degree of variability.

We are now in a position to derive a sales forecast from a forecast of IPI. First, we extend the IPI peak-to-peak diagram using our forecasts for the IPI, and then we produce a sales forecast by multiplying the forecast deviations from trend for the IPI by b to give forecast deviations from trend for forecast sales. Our method therefore continues as follows:

9. Extend the peak-to-peak diagram for the IPI with an IPI forecast. Calculate the peak-to-peak and trough-to-trough lines and thereby extend the trend line (see Figure 8.4).
10. Multiply the forecast IPI deviations by the multiplier b. This gives forecast deviations from trend for sales.
11. Extend the last segment of the sales trend to give a forecast trend. Add to this forecast trend the forecast sales deviations derived in step 10. This gives a sales forecast.

In practice, the whole procedure is sensibly represented and calculated on a PC spreadsheet from which illustrative graphs can be derived.

Very often there is a discontinuity between the end of the sales data and the first forecast point for sales. This is due to the fact that the multiplier b does not remain absolutely

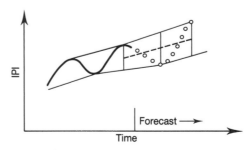

Figure 8.4 Peak-to-peak forecast for the IPI

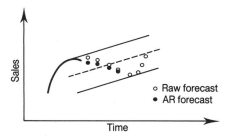

Figure 8.5 Autoregressive modification to peak-to-peak forecast

Table 8.1 Autoregressive modification to peak-to-peak forecast

	IPI	IPI deviation (%)	Sales	Sales deviation (%)	Sales deviation (AR) (%)	Sales (AR)
Actual	101	4.6	123	7.8		
	102	4.5	122	7.2		
	102	4.2	126	9.1	7.8	124
Forecast	101	3.8	124	8.0	7.4	123

constant for the entire run of the data. The normal response is to modify the forecast using the autoregressive structure that we discussed in Chapter 3 in order to smooth out the discontinuity. This is illustrated in Figure 8.5

The mechanism is shown in Table 8.1. The IPI forecasts shown in the first column give rise to percentage sales deviation forecasts shown in column 4, which in turn imply sales forecasts (column 3). These display a clear discontinuity. Column 5 therefore gives column 4 with an autoregressive amendment; these figures are then translated into final sales forecasts in column 6.

The following case study shows how the early stages of the peak-to-peak method can be used for a cyclical product. The data used involve a bulk product — neither the product nor the company involved can be identified for reasons of confidentiality. The case demonstrates some of the difficulties which can be encountered using this method, and how there are areas of subjective judgement which need to be addressed: the method is not totally automatic.

The data in Figure 8.6 are seasonally adjusted and smoothed using the X-11 Henderson curves. It is clearly heavily cyclical, with major peaks in 1973 and 1979 and troughs in 1975 and 1980. The peaks in 1969, 1973, 1979 and 1986 are joined, as are the troughs in 1967, 1975 and 1980. The trough-to-trough line after 1980 is continued parallel to the peak-to-peak line for those years. A number of problem areas become apparent at this stage.

First, we have two consecutive peaks in 1969 and 1973 with no identified intervening trough. This should not normally be the case, although the minor nature of the 1971 trough

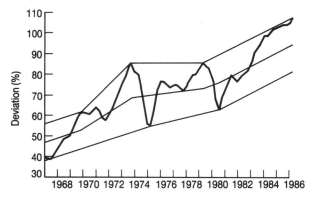

Figure 8.6 Company X volume index

has clearly led the practitioner to omit it from consideration. What is particularly important is that the treatment of prospective peaks and troughs should be identical for both sales and IPI data — as we shall see, this is the case in this instance. This allows the calculation of the multiplier *b* to be carried out under identical circumstances. However, the omission of the 1971 trough has caused the trend to be underestimated for the years around 1971.

Second, there is the difficulty of identifying the final peak, given here as 1986 but which could just as easily have been 1984 or 1985. Company X's product portfolio was changing rapidly in the early 1980s, and this further clouds the issue. The message here is that we need to take account of the peculiarities of our data and make suitable adjustments if necessary. This is particularly true in view of the long runs of data needed to carry out the peak-to-peak method.

Figure 8.7 shows the peak-to-peak diagram for western European industrial production for the same period. (The products in Company X's portfolio are predominantly being sold into Europe.) Again the 1971 trough has been omitted. The less accentuated nature

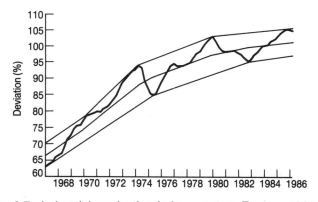

Figure 8.7 Industrial production index, western Europe, 1967–86

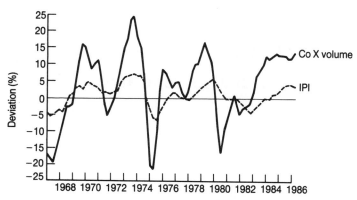

Figure 8.8 Deviations from trend: sales volume and western European industrial production index

of the IPI cycle is apparent. In both Figures 8.6 and 8.7 perpendiculars have been raised and dropped from troughs and peaks in order to estimate the trends. These perpendiculars are not shown on the graphs.

Figure 8.8 shows the deviations from trend of both the volume index and western European industrial production. This demonstrates the highly cyclical nature of the volume index, and also illustrates the fact that the company's volume peaks and troughs are roughly in line with those for industrial production (in terms of timing at least). The only exception is the 1980 trough in sales volume, whereas industrial production only saw a trough in 1982. Since certain peculiarities in Company X's markets were apparent at that time, it was felt that this exception could be ignored and the assumption made for the forecast period that the timing of the cycles for sales volume and industrial production would be identical The multiplier *b* was estimated by eye at 'about 3'. This was because the peaks and troughs were about 3 times the size for sales volume as for industrial production. Forecasts for industrial production were therefore added to Figure 8.7, and deviations from trend calculated and multiplied by 3 to give forecast deviations from trend for sales volume. These were added to a projection of the sales-volume trend, autoregressive modification was carried out due to a slight discontinuity apparent at the end of the historical data, and sales forecasts were thus derived.

CHAPTER 9

Medium-term forecasting 3

Trend-curve analysis

9.1 Non-sinusoidal cycles

So far we have assumed that cyclical movements are roughly sinusoidal in shape — that is, they take the same length of time to rise to a peak as they do to fall to a trough, and they are unimodal, that is, they have single peaks and troughs. In practice, this is often a reasonable assumption, but there are some important exceptions and it is advisable to examine all cycles for this property before embarking on forecasting or planning activities. Two of the more important departures from sinusoidal cycles are described below.

9.1.1 The sawtooth cycle

Figure 9.1 shows a sawtooth cycle. It is so named because it resembles the teeth of a saw, with a rapid rise from trough to peak followed by a more leisurely drop back again. Data series which follow this pattern rarely describe straight lines between peaks and troughs and back again; nevertheless the straight-line model is usually an adequate representation for forecasting and planning purposes since the timing and level of the peaks and troughs are normally of paramount importance rather than the exact path taken between peaks and troughs.

An example of this phenomenon is the unemployment series. Unemployment usually takes about $1\frac{1}{2}$ years to rise from trough to peak and then $3\frac{1}{2}$ years to fall back again. This corresponds to a short sharp involuntary shake-out of labour which is delayed as long as possible into the economic downturn, followed by a cautious re-employment phase as the economy improves. The timing of this sawtooth cycle is shown on the trade-cycle clock in Section 7.6. A method of forecasting medium- to long-term unemployment is shown in Chapter 11.

9.1.2 The bimodal cycle

Sometimes cycles display double peaks or double troughs. In the case of a double peak, a sustained rise occurs, which culminates in an initial peak, after which there is a fall

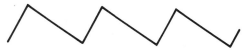

Figure 9.1 The sawtooth cycle

Figure 9.2 The bimodal cycle

which is soon reversed to give a second peak, which is then followed by a steady fall back to the trough. This sequence is shown in Figure 9.2.

Examples of this type of cycle are interest rates and, to a lesser extent, industrial production. The early stages of a cyclical upturn in output are often stimulated by a fall in interest rates (which stimulate the upturn in output through a rapid rebuilding in stock levels, as discussed in Chapter 7). This upturn in stocks is biased towards stocks of raw materials which are often bought in from foreign markets. This destabilizes the balance of payments which in turn causes the currency to fall. This fall can be rapid and requires a rebound in interest rates to prevent a currency collapse. After a while, however, the raw materials are converted into finished products which can be sold in foreign markets, thereby improving the balance of payments again and allowing interest rates to fall. Later in the cycle the growth of output causes demand for money to rise to a point where interest rates have to rise again, and this second rise in interest rates causes destocking (after a lag, as discussed in Chapter 7). Output therefore falls, demand for money diminishes and eventually interest rates fall again, thereby starting the next cycle in output.

Since interest rates affect output through the mechanism of stockbuilding, it is not surprising that this *M*-shaped cycle in interest rates also gives rise to an *M*-shaped cycle in industrial output. However, since stockbuilding is only one of the components of final demand, the effect on output is muted. Normally output starts its cyclical upswing rapidly as restocking takes off, then stabilizes or falls back slightly as the first rise in interest rates reverses the initial restocking. There then follows a final surge in output as the cycle matures, followed by a sustained fall due largely to destocking from an overstretched position. This pattern in industrial production will be repeated in the sales profile for a cyclical product. If the product is heavily cyclical (for example, if the multiplier discussed in Chapter 8 is above 2), then a more noticeable *M*-shape in sales will become apparent. These features can be seen in Figures 8.6 and 8.7 from our case study on peak-to-peak forecasting.

9.2 The product life cycle

This section and the next consider models which relate to both medium- and long-term forecasting.

In the medium term we may well describe sales volume by means of a decomposition model in which the components are short-term seasonality, a trade-cycle term, and a trend which is characterized by a straight line. In the medium term the trend may well be indistinguishable from a straight line. However, as the length of the data set increases we need to be very careful about whether the trend is in fact nonlinear. For example, a medium-term forecast may look only 1–3 years into the future (for which a straight-line trend is adequate), but the forecast may be constructed using 10 years of past data which will probably involve a nonlinear trend. Such a medium-term forecasting model therefore needs to consider long-term trend changes in the data, and to project these changes. In order to do this we need to understand the product life cycle.

Figure 9.3 describes the life cycle for a typical product. Both sales volume and profit levels are graphed. Sales start in the development phase by undergoing slow growth as the emphasis is on trials and not on sales. Profits are usually negative at this stage because of high capital costs and low sales income. The next stage is the growth phase, as the product becomes established and a number of competing companies produce the product. Sales growth is rapid and the product moves into profit. The growth and profitability attracts a large number of potential producers, and in the next stage growth begins to decline (albeit from a high level) and the weakest of the potential producers are squeezed out of the market by the larger producers who, because of economies of scale, continue to make attractive profits. The product then matures and undergoes very slow growth as it stops substituting other products and its markets become saturated. This stage can last a very long time: for many industrial products it can be thought of as everlasting. For example, sulphuric acid production has been growing steadily at around the growth rate of the economy in the UK for over a hundred years. However, it is possible, particularly for consumer goods which are subject to the vagaries of fashion, to enter a final stage where the product declines both in sales and profit terms.

The entire life cycle can be complete in 10 years for some consumer goods. On the other hand, industrial products often take 30 years to reach the beginning of the maturity stage, and this stage can then last at least as long again (and sometimes an indefinite length

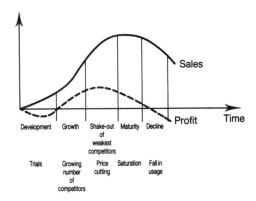

Figure 9.3 The product life cycle

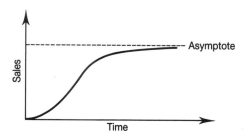

Figure 9.4 Trend for a product with a long maturity stage

of time). In the latter case the long-term trend of such a product will resemble the graph shown as Figure 9.4, eventually flattening out to an asymptotic sales level (or ceiling).

There are a number of mathematical trend curves which describe this graph well, namely the gompertz, logistic and modified exponential curves. We shall meet these again in Section 9.3. However, although Figure 9.4 shows the classical product life cycle for a product with a long maturity stage, in practice it is more common to meet products that grow at the rate of the economy on maturity rather than stopping growing altogether. Typically such a product will end up growing at 3 per cent p.a. rather than standing still. This situation is shown in Figure 9.5.

Unfortunately, it is difficult to model a trend which shows the asymptotic behaviour seen in Figure 9.5. Instead, we normally transform the data so that it reverts to the classical form of Figure 9.4, which we can describe by means of mathematical trend curves. This is done very simply as follows.

If *y* represents sales growing at a rate approaching 3 per cent p.a., and the industrial production index (IPI) is also growing at a trend rate of 3 per cent p.a., then we divide *y* by the IPI and create a new data set of *y*/IPI which will asymptote at 0 per cent p.a. and will resemble the situation shown in Figure 9.4. We are then in a position to fit a mathematical trend curve to the new data set. This curve can be projected to give forecast values of *y*/IPI. We then derive forecast vaues of *y* by multiplying by forecast values of IPI.

As an example, consider Table 9.1, which shows historical sales of 50, 54, 57, ..., and corresponding IPI values of 100, 101, 103, ... Dividing these two sets of data we obtain sales/IPI figures of 0.50, 0.53, 0.55, ... We then fit a trend curve to this data

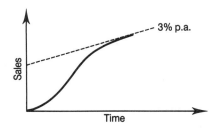

Figure 9.5 Product trend showing typical asymptotic behaviour

Table 9.1   Sales forecast using IPI forecasts

	History				Forecast		
Year	1	2	3	. . .	10	11	. . .
Sales	50	54	57		74	75	
IPI	100	101	103		110	111	
Sales/IPI	0.50	0.53	0.55				
Trend curve	0.49	0.53	0.56		0.67	0.68	

Table 9.2   Sales forecast using a 3 per cent p.a. deflator

	History				Forecast	
Year	1	2	3	. . .	10	11
					. . .	
Sales	50	54	57		74	77
Deflator	1.03	1.061	1.093		1.344	1.384
Deflated sales	48.5	50.0	52.2			
Trend curve	48.2	50.8	52.4		55.2	55.3

set and project it into the forecast region, giving predictions of 0.67, 0.68, ... We can then multiply back by our IPI forecasts (110, 111, . . .) to give forecast sales of 74, 75, ...

This method, of course, presupposes that we are happy with the accuracy of our IPI forecasts. If this is not the case, then we can assume that the product sales will grow at some rate (say, 3 per cent) in the long term, adjust the historical data by dividing by 1.03 raised to some power (for instance, 1.03^9 for the ninth data pont), fitting a trend curve, and multiplying back by the appropriate powers of 1.03 to arrive at a forecast. This would work as in Table 9.2. The same data are used as in the previous example. The deflator is 1.03 raised to the power of the number of the year in question — so, for example, 1.38 = 1.03^{11}. The deflated sales row is obtained by dividing sales by the deflator. So, for example, in year 3 the deflated sales of 52.2 are is 57/1.093. The trend curve is then fitted to the data and projected into the forecast region. These forecasts are then multiplied back by the deflator to give forecast sales. So for example, for year 11 forecast sales of 77 are calculated by 77 = 55.3 × 1.384.

9.3   Trend-curve analysis

As we noted in Section 9.2, the product life cycle which finishes at product maturity with a sales ceiling can be described by a number of mathematical trend curves. Typical trend-curve forecasting packages allow the choice of one of a number of possible trend curves. Many of these curves are mathematically complex and the packages use nonlinear fitting routines to estimate the parameters.

One common trend curve is the straight line given by the expression

$$y = a + bt$$

(Figure 9.6). If y represents sales and t time, this is a relationship between sales and time in which parameters a and b are estimated by least squares to provide the best statistical fit. The straight line is the simplest of the trend curves, and although it is useful for short-term trend extrapolation, it is of more limited use in the long term. The straight line assumes that the sales trend rises by a constant amount each year. This corresponds to a declining growth rate in percentage terms. For example, a sales increase of 10 tonnes per year is a 10 per cent rise if sales are 100 tonnes, but only a 5 per cent increase on sale of 200 tonnes.

A second common trend curve is the parabola:

$$y = a + bt + ct^2$$

(Figure 9.7). This curve allows for curvature in the sales trend, but can be highly dangerous to use in the longer term. This is because a parabola always has a turning point, and although it may describe the onset of maturity well, it will also imply a catastrophic fall in sales immediately after maturity has been reached (see Figure 9.8).

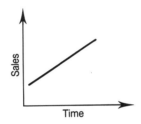

Figure 9.6 Straight-line trend

Figure 9.7 Parabola

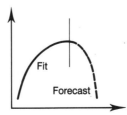

Figure 9.8 Parabola fails to model extended maturity phase

A third trend curve is the exponential, given by

$$\log y = a + bt$$

(Figure 9.9). The exponential curve describes a trend which is growing at a constant rate per annum — for example, a product which is undergoing an extended maturity phase.

The next three trend curves, each involving three parameters, are particularly useful. The additional parameter r falls between 0 and 1 and describes the rate at which maturity is being approached. All three trend curves mimic the product life cycle and assume that the life cycle ends with an extended maturity phase (that is, there is no decline phase). The modified exponential, given by expression

$$y = a - br^t$$

(Figure 9.10) is for products which grow explosively at first, and then approach maturity gradually.

The gompertz curve, with equation

$$\log y = a - br^t$$

(Figure 9.11) reflects relatively slow growth in the early stages in line with the general product life cycle. It is a particularly useful trend curve for describing the sales volume of bulk products.

The logistic curve, written

$$\frac{1}{y} = a + br^t$$

(Figure 9.12) looks very similar to the gompertz, and fits population data very well. However, it is slightly less useful for describing sales-volume data.

A trend-curve analysis computer package will normally fit a range of possible trend

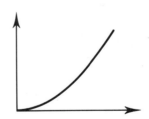

Figure 9.9 Exponential trend curve

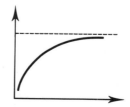

Figure 9.10 Modified exponential trend curve

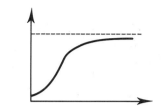

Figure 9.11 Gompertz trend curve

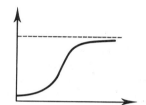

Figure 9.12 Logistic trend curve

curves to the data, and then select the best trend curve by looking for the model with the lowest mean square error. However, this practice only measures which model fits the data best, rather than which model provides the best forecasts. As we have already discussed, it is better to use the out-of-sample forecasting method to select the best model for forecasting purposes. The preferred technique is to fit the various trend curves to the first two-thirds of the sales data and assess which is best by reference to the MSE of the forecasts for the last third of the data. In the author's experience the logistic model is often preferred by in-sample fitting techniques, whereas the suggested out-of-sample method will often prefer the gompertz. Although the logistic and the gompertz look very similar they can throw up quite different forecasts when given the same data.

One of the more difficult parts of trend-curve fitting is estimating the height of the asymptote. This is because the nonlinear fitting routines from which we estimate the parameters for the modified exponential, gompertz and logistic curves have to cope with what are known as difficult response surfaces. If we have some external estimate of the asymptote through market research, for example, then this difficulty disappears because the problem becomes one of linear estimation, for which we can use regression techniques. The three asymptotic trend curves are dealt with as follows.

In the case of the modified exponential, since $y = a - br^t$, y will approach the value a as t tends to infinity (since r lies between 0 and 1). The value a is therefore the asymptote. If we assume that this is known, then we can rewrite the equation as

$$\log(a - y) = \log b + t\log r$$

This is a linear equation which can be estimated by regression.

In the gompertz case $\log y = a - br^t$ which approaches a as t grows large. The asymptote is exp a and we can therefore rewrite the equation as

$$\log(a - \log y) = \log b + t\log r$$

Again this is a linear equation which can be estimated by regression.

In the logistic case, we have $1/y = a + br^t$ which again approaches a as t increases. The asymptote is therefore $1/a$, and, assuming that we know this, we can estimate the other two parameters through the linear regression equation

$$\log\left(\frac{1}{y} - a\right) = \log b + t\log r$$

9.4 Multiple cycle extraction

The peak-to-peak method is useful because it deals with both the amplitude and the phasing (timing) of the cycle. However, there are two circumstances in which we cannot use the peak-to-peak method: first, if there is only a weak relationship between sales and IPI; or second, if the trade cycle is not the only cycle in the data.

An example of the latter problem is in fibres data where sales are affected by a shorter cycle than the trade cycle. This extra cycle causes the former problem to occur as well. A second example, that of the construction cycle, is dealt with more fully in Chapter 10.

If we encounter this problem of multiple cycles, then we need to fit all relevant cycles to the data. Our long-term model thus becomes

$$Y = T + C_1 + C_2 + C_3 + \ldots C_n + E$$

where T is usually a trend curve, C_i are the n cycles and E is the error term. In normal circumstances we would not expect n to exceed 2. Each cycle has its own length, amplitude and phasing. These are illustrated in Figure 9.13.

A cycle can be described by the equation

$$y = a \sin\left(\frac{b + t}{2\pi l}\right)$$

where a is the amplitude, b the phasing and l the length of the cycle. The full model is therefore

$$\log y = a - br^t + a_1\sin\left(\frac{b_1 + t}{2\pi l_1}\right) + a_2\sin\left(\frac{b_2 + t}{2\pi l_2}\right) + \ldots$$

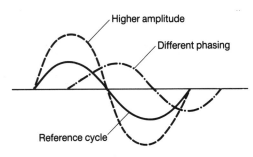

Figure 9.13 Changes in amplitude and phasing

assuming that we are fitting a gompertz curve as the trend. Even with a two-cycle model, we need to estimate nine parameters, which requires a long data series. We can (and normally do) reduce the number of parameters to seven by assuming the length of the two cycles.

A model such as this still suffers from two disadvantages. First, we have assumed constant-amplitude cycles. This is unrealistic, and a variable amplitude will be needed for the forecast (estimated by external studies such as looking at the forecast amplitude of the IPI cycle). Fortunately, the assumption of constant amplitude does not significantly bias the estimates of the other parameters. Second, the estimation of this sort of model is clearly nonlinear, and the response surface of the model is likely to be complicated. It is therefore essential to use high-quality optimization procedures to estimate the parameters. However, despite these difficulties, two-cycle models have been used with some degree of success in the manufacturing sector, and they are particularly useful in cleaning the data (or decycling it) to assess the underlying trend. When both cycles are at a maximum it is all too easy to assume that the underlying trend of the data series is rising faster than in fact it is.

CHAPTER 10

Long-term forecasting 1
The construction cycle

10.1 Introduction

We have already ventured into the long-term forecasting arena by implying that some medium-term considerations such as the trade cycle have important implications for the long-term (over 3 years ahead). This chapter considers a truly long-term feature which is known as the construction cycle. We shall look at the evidence for such a cycle, see how Forrester's system dynamics model explains its presence, and examine its links with demography and how an important sector of the construction market can be forecast relatively accurately.

Figure 10.1 shows how the US housing market performed over the course of a century. The broken line shows a cycle 18 years in length, and its correlation with the actual data is clear. As we shall see later in this chapter, similar cyclical behaviour of the housing market persists after the Second World War and shows signs of increasing in amplitude. Why should such a cycle exist?

10.2 Cause of the construction cycle

To answer this question we return to Forrester's system dynamics model. The trade cycle appears to be caused by the lag between a change in the level of demand for goods and the response of the consumer durables sector in providing labour and stocks to satisfy the new level of demand (as discussed in Chapter 7). Forrester also considered the interaction between the consumer durables sector and the capital equipment sector. A variation in demand on the consumer durables sector may well stimulate a demand for capital equipment by that sector. However, we can expect a lag to occur between the ordering of capital equipment and its delivery, as the capital equipment sector responds to demand on itself. Forrester estimated this lag using available statistical sources for the US economy and discovered, by putting the lag into his model, that a cycle in output of the order of 15–25 years resulted (dependent on the exact value of the lag used). This is consistent with the behaviour of the construction sector in general and the building sector in particular.

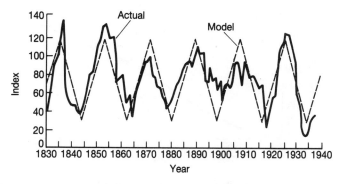

Figure 10.1 Residential building cycle index, USA, 1830–1937

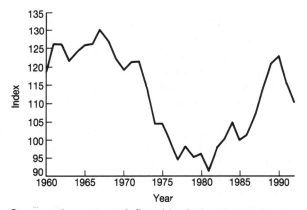

Figure 10.2 Construction output deflated by industrial production, UK, 1960–92

We might expect that this cycle would affect the construction sector more than industrial output generally. The extent to which this is so is illustrated by the data in Figure 10.2 showing the performance of the UK construction sector compared with industrial production. (When the graph moves up, construction output is moving ahead more strongly than industrial output generally, and when the graph moves down construction is relatively weak.) A 7 per cent upturn in the cycle in the 1960s is followed by a decline of no less than 30 per cent in the 1970s. The amplitude of the cycle is therefore highly variable but not negligible.

10.3 The construction cycle and product forecasts

The construction cycle impacts on many sectors outside construction. Any product which has above average exposure to the construction sector will exhibit a cycle in output of the order of 18 years. For example, PVC is a plastic which has many end-uses in the

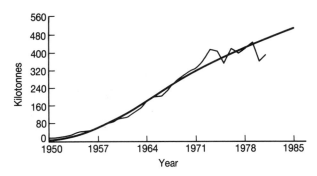

Figure 10.3 UK PVC market

construction sector. In 1982 the UK market was plotted from 1950 to 1981 to obtain the graph in Figure 10.3. A gompertz life cycle curve was fitted to the data, shown by the smooth curve passing through the middle of the data. The residuals from the gompertz can be seen to be above the curve for a sequence of years then below for several years, then above and so on. The periods for which the residuals are negative correspond to the low part of the construction cycle and positive residuals correspond to the high part of the construction cycle.

The importance of the cycle is highlighted by observing that PVC growth, at over 20 per cent p.a. during the 1960s when the construction cycle was moving upwards, suddenly disappeared altogether for most of the 1970s as a steep construction cycle downturn took place. Major players in the marketplace were taken by surprise by this sudden change as plants which had been constructed in the late 1960s, on the assumption that annual growth of 10 per cent would continue, were found not to be needed. Sharply reduced prices and profits resulted. Much of the blame was laid at the door of the oil crisis of 1973−4 and the resulting recession in 1975, but subsequent analysis showed that the flattening off in the market started well before the oil crisis (a simple 5-year moving average through the data makes this point quite well). As a result of this misunderstanding of the role of the construction cycle in the industry, older PVC plants were scrapped and the upturn in the fortunes of PVC in the 1980s as the construction cycle turned up again nearly embarrassed the slimmed-down industry as PVC growth returned to very healthy levels!

10.4 Housebuilding

Figure 10.4 shows housebuilding starts in Great Britain since the Second World War. This can be seen to follow the construction series fairly closely, although housebuilding is only one of several components within total construction. We shall now develop a non-cyclical forecast for this important sector. The reasons for doing this are twofold: to check whether housebuilding is likely to continue to follow the construction cycle; and to propose a general forecasting method which can be useful in forecasting other sectors.

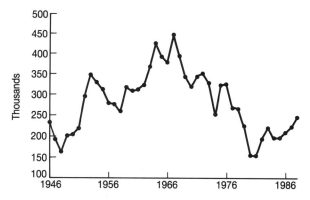

Figure 10.4 Housebuilding starts, Great Britain, 1946–88

The housing stock held by a particular country is subject to certain major forces. On the supply side, the housing stock can be increased by new building or reduced by demoliton. The net increase in housing stock in any particular year is thus the difference between new building and demolition. On the other hand, there are demand pressures on the housing stock. Demand will be increased by the number of new families formed in a given year and requiring housing. Conversely, demand is decreased by the death of any person forming a single-person household; this releases housing back into the system. These changes are summarized in Figure 10.5. Note that we are assuming that all dwellings are included in the definition of housing.

If we can forecast the number of new families and the number of deaths, then we can also forecast the net increase in the housing stock. If we also assume a forecast for demolition rates, then the supply equation will imply a forecast for new housebuilding. It must be emphasized that there are other factors to be taken into account such as the number of second homes required, but these are minor factors and the method outlined above is quite sufficient to give a good directional model for housebuilding. In addition, as we shall see, no statistical estimation is required for this model and therefore there is no statistical error

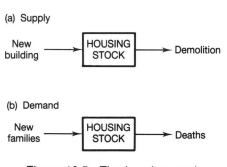

Figure 10.5 The housing stock

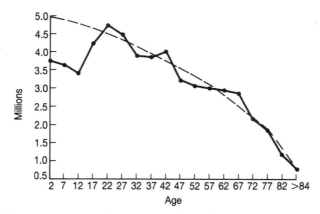

Figure 10.6   Population of the UK by age, 30 June 1988

arising from the forecasting technique. Statistical error can be very substantial in some forecasting techniques, so removing this form of error is a major advantage.

Let us take a look at the population profile for the UK in order to indicate how many new families we can expect in the future. The age distribution of the UK population is shown in Figure 10.6. The numbers of people are measured in 5-year age bands. For example, 'age 7' on the horizontal axis refers to the number of people between the ages of 5 and 9 inclusive. It is clear that although there is the expected decline with age indicated by the broken line, there are also major deviations from that trend as the birth rate has increased and fallen at various stages in the past.

For example, there is a clear peak at age 42. This corresponds to the postwar baby boom. The peak at age 22 is an echo of the postwar baby boom as the babies grew up and had their own babies in the 1960s. The most obvious deviation from trend, however, occurs between ages 22 and 12. This sudden drop reflects the massive fall in the birth rate during the 1970s, a fall which has since been only partially reversed. This sudden decline in the birth rate has implications for the housing market, and indeed for many other markets.

Before we move on to the housing forecast, let us briefly consider other uses to which this data set can be put. The value of demographic data is that anyone who has been born will in 10 years' time be 10 years older, assuming that he/she does not die before then. So, for example, if the birth rate has declined for the last 5 years, then there will be less pressure on school provision as we can confidently forecast a decline in children of school age over the following 10 years. Similarly, a bulge in the population between ages 10 and 15 means upward pressure on unemployment 5−10 years ahead (all other things being equal). This latter argument was used by ICI in the mid-1970s, when UK unemployment was 1.5 million, to forecast that unemployment would rise to around 3 million by 1980, and that this would be reflected in easier recruitment conditions for the company. In general, if a product sells into an age-specific market, then demographic analysis is needed to forecast demand accurately. Similarly, targeting of new products should often be done with the size of the recipient population in mind.

In order to forecast the number of new family units, let us focus on the population aged 20−24. This is a rough average age at which young people might move away from parental accommodation. We know the number of people in that age group in the past, and we can project the number into the future. For example, in 5 years' time the number of 20−24-year-olds will be approximately equal to the number of 15−19-year-olds now. There will be a slight difference due to deaths and net immigration, but for the purposes of this study these differences are too small to worry about. We can now convert our historical and forecast numbers of 20−24-year-olds to differences between 5-year periods. Table 10.1 illustrates this. For example, the number of 20−24-year-olds rose by 645 000 between 1962 and 1967 (this represents the postwar baby boom). On the other hand, the next 5-year period saw a decline of 38 000 20−24-year-olds. The table shows how the number of 20−24-year-olds oscillates wildly (there are only around 4 million people in this age group, so changes of up to 20 per cent in magnitude take place in a 5-year period in the population aged 20 to 24).

The figures also show an interesting pattern. The rise in the 1960s is followed by a fall in the 1970s, a rise in the 1980s, followed by a considerable fall in the 1990s as the fall in the birth rate in the 1970s carries through to a new generation of potential parents. The construction cycle has also risen and fallen in line with these changes in the number of young adults in the past — the figures for the 1990s suggest that the cycle will continue until the early years of the twenty-first century at least. This is true for the housebuilding sector of construction, and in the past the overall construction cycle has followed the direction of housebuilding in the medium and long term. The figures for the mid to late 1990s look particularly threatening — what we now need is a rough forecast of actual housebuilding arising from these population figures.

It is important to realize that although there are many minor considerations involved in a housing forecast (such as death rates, immigration and family size) the major determinant of new housing requirements is the shift in the number of young people. Thus a directional model for the housing market can be obtained by concentrating solely on the main factor, and this directional forecast will be quite sufficient to drive strategy considerations for the building industry and its suppliers.

A forecast for UK housebuilding is given in Table 10.2. The top row gives the UK population of young adults — the actual figures historically and forecasts using the latest data. The second row gives the current death rate, together with forecasts which assume that the current death rate will remain unchanged for the foreseeable future. (This is roughly in line with recent changes in the death rate.) Subtracting these two figures, we obtain the net number of new adults over each 5-year period. So far we have been working in 5-year time bands. We therefore have to divide by 5 to derive the net number of new adults per annum. This number has to be converted into households. Suppose that there is an average of 1.6 people per household in the population aged 20−24 in the households where deaths occur; we divide the annual figure for net new adults by 1.6 to find the annual figure of net new households. Although the factor 1.6 is declining slowly, the forecast is not sensitive to small deviations in this number so an unchanged factor of 1.6 has been used throughout the forecast.

On top of the net number of new households we also have to take account of non-

Table 10.1 UK
demographic data

5 years ending	Additional 20—24-year-olds (thousands)
1967	643
1972	−38
1977	−44
1982	531
1987	350
1992	−400
1997	−900
2002	30

Table 10.2 UK housebuilding forecast (thousands)

	1989	1994	1999	2004
UK population (20—24-year-olds)	4650	4080	3380	3630
Deaths (×5)	3250	3250	3250	3250
Net new adults	1400	830	130	380
Net new adults (p.a.)	280	166	26	76
Net new households	175	104	16	48
Non-demographic demand	45	45	45	45
Housebuilding	220	149	61	93

demographic demand. This arises from slum clearance, the rising need for second homes and other factors. In the recent past this has averaged around 45 000 per year, and although it could vary considerably in response to changes in government spending policies, for example, it seems reasonable to assume an unchanged figure through the forecast years as a base case. Adding the number of new households to non-demographic demand, we can obtain a forecast for new housebuilding requirements. This forecast underlines the effect of the plunge in birth rate in the 1970s, implying a sudden onset of tough times for builders in the 1990s and very little relief in later years. Rationalization in the housebuilding sector looks highly likely.

Many European countries share the same profile of a sudden decline in the number of young adults in the 1990s, thus their experiences of the pressure on housebuilding are likely to be similar. Accepting the demographic underpinning of the forecast, the fact that so many European countries share the same demographic profile is not really surprising. The postwar baby boom was a root cause of the downturn in birth rates in the 1970s (in direction, if not amplitude) and the war affected all European countries. Interestingly, the country with the largest decline in births in the 1970s was West Germany, and it is therefore West Germany which is most at risk due to the knock-on effects in the 1990s. It remains to be seen which country adapts its strategy best to the changing circumstances.

10.5 Impact of demographic swings

The sort of demographic analysis which we have carried out here can be used for a variety of problems. Typical areas in which demographic analysis leads to important strategic decisions include the following:

Housing: This may be analyzed as above, strategic implications for the building sector, its suppliers and the government.

Human resource planning in companies: Models simulating the changing age distribution of the company under various proposed recruitment policies and assuming various (age-dependent) wastage rates should be used by all large companies to test the personnel implications of various strategic moves. For example, we can examine the long-term effects of a few years of zero recruitment and early retirement options. In addition, demographic analysis gives a forecast of pressures on unemployment and therefore ease of recruitment, via a study of the number of 15−19-year-olds projected to come on to the labour market over the next 10 years or so.

Automobiles: The types of model to be sold should reflect the age distribution of potential buyers. The size of the market will also depend on the number of potential buyers weighted according to age.

Consumer durables: Many durables are sold according to the age of the buyer. For example, household durables are largely bought when a couple is setting up home (in their early twenties, say), and in middle age when the children have left home. Producers of such items can therefore project the number of people in those age ranges and use this as an input to their long-term forecasts and plans.

Industrial products: An important type of forecast for industrial products is end-use analysis. This can lead to a demographic input. An example already described is that of PVC, for which the construction sector accounts for around 50% of sales either directly or indirectly (in items which are part of a house or items which are used in a house).

Education: Demographic analysis gives important early warning of pressures likely to arise in education, or other age-related sectors. A strategic response can then be thought out to counter or to take into account these pressures.

Capital expenditure: A global or European business will often site new plant close to the potential markets, especially if margins are tight and/or freight charges are high. Although there are many other strategic influences, demographic analysis will point to suitable countries in which to site a plant according to availability of labour in the longer term (by analyzing the number of 15−19-year-olds) as well as demographic influences on market size, as discussed above.

Finally a word of warning. It is very important to make sure that any long-term forecast uses variables which are useful long-term predictors. Some predictors are useful in the short term, but fail to perform adequately in the longer term. Demographic variables are always long-term in nature, and will need the addition of other variables in order to describe

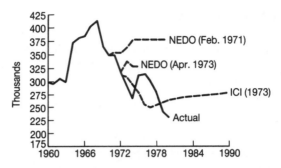

Figure 10.7 House completions, Great Britain, since 1960

short- and medium-term phenomena such as the trade cycle. If the direction of the trend is all that is needed, however, then demographic data will often score over economic information. An example of how *not* to do it is shown in Figure 10.7. In 1970 the British housing market had fallen for two successive years. In 1971 the National Economic Development Organization (NEDO) made a long-term forecast of house building which said that interest rates were high, but were expected to fall; that interest rates affect housebuilding; therefore that housebuilding would recover over the next 4 years before levelling out, reflecting interest-rate expectations.

Unfortunately, housebuilding continued to fall. Two years later, NEDO made another forecast using similar methodology. Again the predicted recovery was notable for its absence. At the same time ICI made an internal trend forecast using demographic methods. The result can be seen in Figure 10.7. Although, as discussed above, the forecast failed to pick out medium-term fluctuations around the trend, the ICI forecast gave a much more useful picture than that of NEDO. The important factor is that while interest rates do indeed give a useful *short-term* forecast of building activity, their usefulness is non-existent in the long term due to the relative importance of truly long-term effects such as demography. A further warning should be sounded against the use of models using only economic data at the expense of socio-economic information.

CHAPTER 11

Long-term forecasting 2
The long wave

11.1   Introduction

So far, we have studied two cycles which can affect business forecasts: the 5-year trade cycle and the 18-year construction cycle. In addition to these two there is also a very long-term cycle which can have significant effects on very long-range strategic planning. For this reason it is probably of most interest to central or strategic planning departments rather than to product planning departments. It can be used to help determine the environment in which a company shape strategy can be built up. In addition, it has something to say about the changing nature of trade cycles dependent on the phase of this long-term cycle.

The long wave is indeed a wave rather than a cycle — it rises slowly before collapsing in a potentially catastrophic manner. Its length is 50–60 years, and it is associated with the Russian economist Kondratieff and his pioneering work in the 1920s. The length of the wave means that relatively few cycles of data are available for analysis, and therefore conclusions based on statistical methodology alone must be treated with caution. Fortunately, as we shall see, other methods of analysis support the contention that such a wave should exist. Kondratieff's prediction that a period of economic austerity would occur towards the end of the twentieth century has also stood the test of time.

The long wave primarily affects prices, profits and hence unemployment rather than volume, although some sectors such as the capital equipment sector will see substantial movements in sales volume. Figure 11.1 shows the price of copper in constant dollars since 1800. Comparison with the long-term downward trend of this series shows peaks around 1800, 1850, 1920 and 1970, along with intervening troughs. We can also see the generally steady rise in the peaks, but a rapid fall once those peaks have been established.

11.2   Causes of the long wave

A number of hypotheses have been put forward to explain the existence of the long wave. Unfortunately, the absence of many data series of sufficient length to test these hypotheses statistically leaves a question-mark over their veracity. We have already seen, however, that simulation models can examine the effect of relatively short economic lags in producing

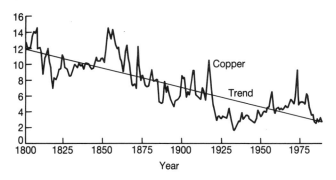

Figure 11.1 Copper prices in constant dollars, 1800−1989

longer cycles. In particular, we have examined the use of Forrester's system dynamics model in our study of the trade and construction cycles. Forrester used the same model to draw conclusions about the cause of the long wave.

He began by verifying that insertion of the various lags that the model identifies does indeed produce a long wave of 50−60 years in length. The question remains as to which is the relationship within the model responsible for triggering a long wave. Forrester isolated the vital area as the capital equipment sector. The trade cycle depends on lags between market demand and the response of the consumer durables sector. The construction cycle depends on the lags between demand from the consumer durables sector and the response of the capital equipment sector. In addition, Forrester noted that output from the capital equipment sector tended to show a cycle of 50−60 years of significant proportions.

Figure 11.2 illustrates the way the capital equipment sector shrinks and expands over the course of the long wave. The sector's capacity is low at the trough of the long wave (say, in 1950), and is insufficient to satisfy underlying trend demand. The sector can only build up its capacity slowly and it is not until point X on the graph that capacity and demand are back in line. By this stage there is a backlog of unfulfilled orders, and so the sector continues to expand its capacity until at some point Y (say, 1970) it is perceived that capacity

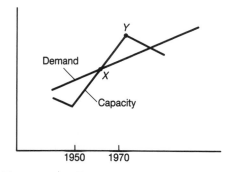

Figure 11.2 The capital equipment sector

and demand are out of line and a correction takes place. Forrester's contribution was in identifying that the important determinant of the long wave was the so-called *feedback loop* in the capital equipment sector. The capital equipment sector has to produce capital equipment for itself. Therefore when demand for capital equipment rises and the capital equipment sector needs to expand to satisfy the new higher level of demand, the first thing the sector must do is to produce more equipment for itself. This necessarily reduces its capacity to meet outside demand at the very time it is needed the most. Thus the shortage of capital equipment as seen by the consumer durables sector appears to deteriorate before it improves.

Forrester experimented by eliminating the feedback loop in his model. He did this by creating a hypothetical sector which could supply the capital equipment sector with equipment when it needed it. He found that this was sufficient to eliminate the long wave from the output of the model. The existence of a feedback loop for the capital equipment sector is therefore the reason for the existence of a long wave.

11.3   Milestones in the long wave

It is possible to construct a clock similar to the trade-cycle clock (Section 7.6) in order to illustrate the economic milestones that we can expect to pass as the long wave progresses. If we start at the lowest stage of the long wave, then the most significant feature for the business executive is the low capital base which follows a sustained period of economic adversity featuring weak selling prices, low profits and a difficult financial climate. This stage was seen in the 1930s. We then pass into a long period of expansion (as in the 1950s and 1960s) in which industrial capacity is steadily built up, prices and profits gradually improve and volume growth is somewhat above the long-term trend. Unfortunately, the later stages of the expansion involve an overexpansion of industry above the long-term trend of demand. This creates rising corporate and country debt, and servicing that debt is only simple under the assumptions of a continuing growth in sales volume and profitability. A further symptom of the later stages of the expansion is the gradual increase of inflation.

Most governments will eventually attack accelerating inflation with increased monetary stringency (as in the UK in 1974–5). This has the side-effect of reducing production growth and increasing unemployment. Companies respond to a situation of high capacity and low demand by cutting prices and thereby reducing profitability. In severe cases, where capacity has been built up in anticipation of a continuation of growth and profitability as experienced in the upturn, capacity is scrapped and many mergers take place as businesses seek to reduce their exposure to products which are now making a loss. This was taking place in the late 1970s and early 1980s. Finally, the debts which were run up in the upturn will turn bad in many cases, leading to pressure on the financial institutions, in response to which they will only lend on the basis of very solid expenditure proposals. This all conspires to produce an industrial sector with a low capital base ready for the next upswing. This last phase of the downswing is the stage where financial collapse is most likely. It can result in the collapse of large sections of the world financial system, as in 1929–30, or

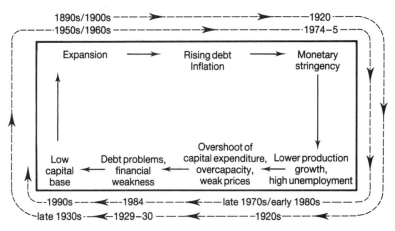

Figure 11.3   Economic changes within a Kondratieff cycle

just a long period of debt write-offs by that system as in the 1980s and early 1990s. Figure 11.3 shows a long-wave clock reported in ICI in 1974. Subsequent events have supported the timing proposed here, and so the next upswing should start in the early years of the twenty-first century.

11.4   Innovation and the long wave

One of the results of the long wave is the bunching of the births of new innovations at the low point of the wave. Many old industries reach maturity as the long wave turns down, and the deterioration of profitability in these businesses leads to an unacceptable increase in debt. Banks, already under pressure, will be unwilling to finance these businesses further, and will look much more kindly on innovative products which will enjoy relatively high growth and, because they are new, have no inherited debt to write off. Innovative businesses are therefore much more likely to attract capital at the trough of the long wave than during the upturn of the wave when existing sectors will still be exhibiting strong growth and profitability.

Mensch (1979) proposed a metamorphosis model to describe this process, in which new industries rise from the ashes of the old. He illustrated this concept by means of the schematic diagram shown in Figure 11.4. Major innovations at previous long-wave troughs

Figure 11.4   Mensch's metamorphosis theory

include textiles, iron and steam power around 1820; railroadization around 1870; electricity, cars and television around 1930; and microelectronics and biotechnology in the 1980s.

11.5 The 1975 slump

One of the important uses of the long wave is to identify key turning points in economic history, and not to overemphasize short-term influences. An excellent example concerns the recession experienced in 1975. The 1950s and 1960s had seen good volume growth, low unemployment, low inflation and a relatively muted amplitude to the trade cycle. By the early 1970s no severe recession had been experienced in the UK since the Second World War. However, inflation was stirring towards the end of the 1960s as the long wave upturn neared its peak. In 1973—4 the first oil crisis occurred, and in 1975 a severe recession followed. Not surprisingly, the two events were linked, and it was initially believed that the severity of the recession was entirely due to the increase in oil prices. However, more considered economic modelling in the late 1970s ascribed only a fairly small part of the 1975 downturn to the effect of the oil price rise. In any case, if the oil price hike were the only determinant of the 1975 experience, then that effect should have fed through the economic system by the late 1970s, leading to a resumption of growth as normally seen in a cyclical upturn. This failed to materialize.

The 1975 slump was due to the timing of the long wave. As van Duijn (1983) explains, the long wave was approaching its peak because US growth recession had been under way since 1973; inflation had been rising world-wide since the mid-1960s; US, UK, West German and French growth had been slowing since the mid-1960s; profit rates had been declining since the mid-1960s; stock markets had signalled a downturn since mid-1972; and structural unemployment had been rising since the mid-1960s.

The year 1975 was very similar to 1921, when the monetary brakes were applied, thereby reducing inflation, growth and increasing unemployment throughout the 1920s. An ICI report written in 1974, based largely on analysis of the long wave, predicted the extent of the 1975 recession and the austerity of the following years. For instance, although UK unemployment was only 0.5 million in 1974, successful forecasts were made that it would reach 1.5 million by 1976 and 3 million five years later. The accepted wisdom at the time was that it would be politically impossible for unemployment to exceed 1 million!

11.6 Business responses

Although the long wave is so long that it appears to be of little use in business planning, this is not the case. Our discussion of the year 1975 shows, for example, how we can add useful knowledge to our forecast of one particular year by using the long wave. The main use of long-wave theory, however, is in strategic planning in the medium to longer term.

For example, early in the upswing (as in the 1950s and early 1960s) businesses should

- increase capacity well in advance of need (product growth is assured and the capital equipment sector will be struggling to satisfy demand and there may be delays)
- reduce cash and increase borrowing;
- build stocks;
- increase market share aggressively (the cost of doing this in a high-growth, high-profit environment will be relatively low);
- service the innovative new industries (concentrate resources on satisfying demand from the industries which have risen from the ashes of the last long-wave trough).

Late in the upswing (as in the late 1960s and early 1970s), they should

- increase capacity conservatively (anticipate lower sales growth);
- increase cash and reduce borrowing;
- reduce stocks;
- consolidate existing market share;
- ditch struggling businesses and suspend acquisitions.

When the wave breaks (as in the late 1970s, 1980s and early 1990s), they should

- avoid debt-sensitive markets;
- expect low growth;
- expect large trade-cycle swings;
- anticipate new technology and/or new markets, and restructure business to satisfy these in the upswing;
- maintain high cash and low stocks.

11.7 Combinations of cycles

We have discussed, in the last few chapters, three cycles which affect business life: the trade cycle; the construction cycle; and the long wave. As Schumpeter (1939) explained, it is sensible to see what the net result of these cycles is when they are combined.

Take, for example, the 1970s. The long wave was just entering its downswing, and the decade also saw a marked downturn in the construction cycle. A sharp deterioration in business climate was the result. On the other hand, the 1980s, while still depressed in terms of the long wave, saw an upswing in the construction cycle, and the net result of these influences was a decade of higher growth albeit with a continued debt problem and high unemployment. The 1990s look likely to incorporate a substantial downturn in the construction cycle with continued depression in terms of the long wave, and will therefore see a return to generally difficult business conditions until the later years of the decade at least. On the other hand, the early years of the twenty-first century should feature a gentle rise in the construction cycle (due largely to demographic influences already in place), and a resumption of growth in the long wave. Added together, this should result in the best climate for the business community for some time.

A similar analysis (examining the sum of the construction cycle and the long wave) gives us clues as to the nature of the trough of the long wave. We might expect to see a bad recession as the monetary brakes are applied in the early stages of the long-wave downturn (as in 1921 and 1975). The resultant pressure on the financial institutions could cause a crisis at some stage later on (as in 1929−30). Whether or not that crisis can be averted may depend on whether the construction cycle is providing any assistance at that stage of the long wave. A financial crisis was most likely in the current long wave in the mid-1980s (about ten years after the initial monetary correction). However, the pressure was lessened by the fact that the construction cycle was moving up during the 1980s, and a full-blown crisis was averted. Unfortunately, the opposite was the case in 1929−30 and the bolstering of a long-wave crisis point with a construction downturn helped produce the financial crash that followed. Again, the long wave downturn in the 1870s and 1880s turned out just to be a long dull period rather than a financial crisis because of the fact that the construction cycle was turning up when the financial crisis was most likely.

Finally, we must comment on the nature of the trade cycle during the weaker years of the long wave. These years usually involve historically high real interest rates. These high interest rates, taken together with the more fragile nature of the business world, will invoke a greater likelihood of companies destocking heavily during trade-cycle troughs. This means that those troughs will often be particularly marked. For this reason the trade cycle exhibits a higher amplitude on average in the weak years of the long wave than during the upturn. It is, therefore, particularly important that companies anticipate downturns in the trade cycle during the trough of the long wave and apply corrections in stock policy in good time.

11.8 Forecasting using the long wave

We have already seen how a rough knowledge of the long-wave clock, together with acknowledgement of the phasing of the construction cycle, can be used to anticipate business developments in long-term forecasting. It is important, however, to use this information as an environmental backcloth upon which we can paint a more detailed picture.

For example, suppose we wanted to make a long-term forecast of UK unemployment in order to anticipate human resource pressures in industry. Unemployment is the difference between the employable workforce and the working population. To estimate the working population we need a forecast for industrial growth. This can be thought of as the sum of trend growth and a (trade) cyclical factor. Suppose we are forecasting from 1974 (take, for example, the forecast described in Section 11.5). We can anticipate that we are about to enter a depressed phase of the long wave. Trend growth will therefore rise by (say) 2.5 per cent p.a. Using the past relationship between growth and the working population, we would therefore forecast that the trend in the working population would fall a little. On top of this trend is the trade-cycle effect. In 1974 we were close to the peak of a trade cycle in terms of working population (the cyclical peak for production has passed and employment tends to lag behind production). Knowing where we are in the trade cycle, we can therefore estimate the starting point for the working population trend by taking the known current working population figure and subtracting the effect of the current cyclical peak. This gives a starting point as in Figure 11.5.

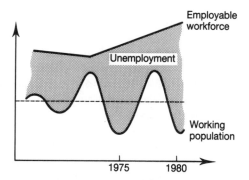

Figure 11.5   Forecast for unemployment made in 1974

We can then extend the working population trend to decline slightly (the exact figures derived from statistical analysis of past data). On top of this can be superimposed a cyclical effect — a large-amplitude cycle was used in this particular forecast, partly due to the fact that we are in the depressed phase of the long wave and can therefore expect large-amplitude cycles fairly frequently. Thus we have derived a forecast for the working population. The employable workforce can be estimated entirely from demographic data. Basically the major effect in producing changes in the employable workforce is the change in the number of school and university leavers. This can be forecast from the number of young teenagers at present. There are other factors, such as changes in the female participation rate, but relatively speaking this effect will be small over the time period considered. In any forecasting exercise it is important to ignore relatively small effects, since the statistical errors introduced by including such variables negate the usefulness of the factor itself. 'Keep it simple' is a vital forecasting maxim. The forecast for unemployment is now derived by subtracting the working population forecast from the employable workforce forecast. As in the case of the housing forecast considered in Chapter 10, we can accept the fact that our forecast is not precise, but it is accurate enough for useful strategic decisions to be taken. The conclusion in this case was that UK unemployment would rise significantly and therefore difficulties experienced in 1974 in recruiting good-quality personnel would rapidly diminish. As described in Section 11.5, the forecast was that unemployment would rise from 0.5 million in 1974 to around 3 million in 1980. If the actual rise was only to 2.5 million or even 2 million, this would not affect the recruitment strategy implied by the forecast. Extreme accuracy was not required.

CHAPTER 12

Long-term forecasting 3
Delphi, scenarios and shocks

12.1 Introduction

In any form of forecasting we have to accept that there will be potentially large confidence intervals around our best forecasts. It is possible to deal with this entirely statistically, and to construct 95 per cent confidence intervals assuming that our underlying model is correct and that none of the assumptions underlying that model is violated. Unfortunately, these assumptions are seldom realistic in modelling real-world problems. Calculated confidence intervals commonly underestimate actual confidence intervals in the forecast region by a factor of 3 or 4. For this reason non-statistical methods have been developed to make long-term forecasts and to assess the likely variability around these forecasts. This chapter deals with the Delphi technique and the scenario approach. In addition, we shall consider how to forecast step changes in the economic world, and how these step changes might be used as an input to product or company forecasts.

12.2 The Delphi technique

The Delphi technique tends to be used for very long-term forecasts of the environment in which our company will be operating. It can be used to assess which products will be in demand in the long term, and therefore is a useful strategic planning tool in determining the optimum long-term shape of the company. It commonly precedes research planning where we try to isolate useful directions in which we should be concentrating our research effort, and portfolio analysis in the business planning area where we try to see how the long-term future, with several new products, can be supported by the cash and profit contributions of ageing but still viable product groups. This area of portfolio analysis is a large subject in its own right, and the reader is referred to the many texts in this area, including Abell and Hammond (1979) and Johnson and Scholes (1988).

The aim of the Delphi technique is to obtain a consensus about the future, using a group of experts. When using a panel of experts it is important to minimize the undesirable aspects of group interaction. For example, the group may have a dominant individual whose views achieve a disproportionate weighting solely due to the force of his/her personality. The

Delphi technique minimizes this effect. In addition, an attempt is made to eliminate committee activity and therefore the 'bandwagon' effect. Letters are used for communication to further this aim.

An example of a wide-ranging Delphi activity might involve the question 'What inventions and scientific breakthroughs are urgently needed and could be achieved in the next 20 years?' In the first phase of the technique a letter would be sent to all experts on the panel posing this question. Responses would be sent back to the co-ordinator, who would derive a list of either all responses or the responses of most interest to the company in question.

In the second phase the experts would be asked (for each item) when the breakthrough could be expected. Responses might take the form of a choice of one of four 5-year bands: the breakthrough will occur 0–5 years ahead, 6–10 years ahead, 11–15 years ahead, or 16–20 years ahead. Again the co-ordinator would collate the replies and construct charts showing, for each potential breakthrough, their distribution.

In the third phase a further letter would be sent to the panel of experts, showing the charts constructed at the end of the second phase, but splitting these charts into consensus items involving a relatively low spread of responses, and non-consensus items where the spread was larger. In each case the average, the lower quartile and the upper quartile would be given. Experts who gave divergent answers would be asked either to justify them or to reassess their answers.

The fourth phase is a repeat of the third phase in which the charts are updated to reflect the changes made by the experts in that third phase. Again, the experts may wish to modify their positions in view of the changed views of the other experts, or (more likely) the explanations given for divergent views by the other experts.

The end result is a list of consensus items which the company can use to assess the implications for its own product types. This will imply useful areas in which the company should proceed with research, and give a valuable input to the strategic planning process.

12.3 Scenarios

The Delphi technique gives an idea of several possible futures. The scenario approach explores the impact of these possible futures on the company. The time-scale for scenario planning is still long-term, but is often less long-term than for the Delphi technique. It concerns the transition to a new long-term position rather than the final position itself. It can also be used to model the effects of various possible economic scenarios on company performance.

Shell pioneered the use of scenario methods in the UK, and an example of that company's analysis is given below. Shell's concern in 1980 was to forecast the long-term future for UK oil consumption. The company accepted that this would depend to a large extent on the general thrust of economic management in the UK. The economists were divided on the likely path forward, and so Shell considered the effects of three scenarios.

Scenario 1 was dubbed 'Unresolved conflicts'. This involved the government muddling through: responding to short-term economic pressures and ignoring medium- and long-term planning. This would reflect the economic management seen in the 1960s and 1970s. In these circumstances it was likely that oil demand would increase slightly.

Scenario 2 was called 'Revival'. This involved a major restructuring of industry in which mature sectors would be wound down and major new industries would be encouraged. These new industries would contribute to a higher level of economic growth. However, these new industries would almost certainly incorporate energy-saving technology, so that growth in output would not necessarily lead to a corresponding growth in oil usage. 'Revival' is what one might expect at some stage of the trough of the Kondratieff wave which we discussed in Chapter 11.

Scenario 3 was named 'Rake's progress'. This involved a persistent changing of economic policies (perhaps reflecting changes of government) in which no one strategy was given time to work. This would give rise to low GDP growth, but would also include the retention of mature energy-intensive industries, so that oil demand would increase in line with GDP. This scenario differs from scenario 1 in that scenario 1 involves a single economic policy which is short-term in nature, whereas scenario 3 includes a number of rapidly changing policies.

The company could now identify contingency plans which would be used in the event of any one of these scenarios occurring. There would undoubtedly be a favourite scenario, and initial plans would be laid to take the greatest advantage of this scenario. However, the situation would be under constant scrutiny so that as soon as one of the other scenarios looked like taking place, the relevant contingency plans could be put into action. The need to monitor developments is central to the operation of scenario planning, and indeed a major updating exercise on the available scenarios would take place every few years. The detailed implications for all the company's products would proceed via a company planning model (see Chapter 18) in which each scenario would be translated into macro-economic and other environmental assumptions, and these would be translated into product sales and profit forecasts via suitable models.

12.4 Example: the scenario approach to planning for shocks

One useful outlet for scenario planning is to allow an assessment of the possible results of a major environmental shock to the system. It is often (but not always) possible to predict a step change in some economic variable of interest to the company. However, it is usually very difficult to forecast the extent of the step change. The scenario approach can be used in these circumstances to model the effects of various sizes of step change. The following example shows how this can be done, and reflects work done in ICI during the early and mid-1980s.

The industrialized world suffered two step changes upwards in the world oil price in the 1970s. By the early 1980s the oil price settled around $30 per barrel, and the accepted wisdom was that the price would increase in the future at a rate several percentage points above the rate of inflation. In other words, oil would become steadily more expensive compared with other industrial materials. As often happens, the step changes upwards had built in expectations of further upward moves. However, the fundamentals were moving against the oil producers and so an analysis of the oil price was carried out.

12.4.1   The prediction of a step change in oil prices

The analysis which was carried out was simple both statistically and in terms of the depth of analysis of the oil industry itself. This is in accord with the maxim 'Keep it simple' which all forecasters do well to heed. The starting point was to analyze the linkage between world oil usage and industrial production. Before the first oil crisis in the mid-1970s these two factors moved in parallel with each other.

However, the steep rise in the price of oil stimulated the industrial world to identify and implement ways of reducing the usage of oil. This involved initiatives across the spectrum of industrial activity. For instance, electricity power generation moved away from the use of oil as a raw material towards coal, gas and nuclear technology. New car models were built with smaller and more effecient engines giving rise to lower petrol consumption. Manufacturing industry spent large amounts of money on accelerating the move to technology which involved considerably lower oil consumption. Individuals no longer installed oil-fired central heating.

The effect of this change in attitude was only felt over a considerable number of years. People only changed to a new more efficient car when their existing one wore out. The owners of oil-fired central heating systems continued to run them — the installation of new non-oil systems only became a major factor after a number of years. As a result the linkage between world oil production and world industrial production continued to be close during the mid-1970s, as can be seen from Figure 12.1. However, thereafter the weight of energy-conservation measures made itself felt, and oil production started to trend downwards despite an upward trend in world industrial production. Given that the 1979 oil price rise had the effect of underpinning and extending existing energy-conservation

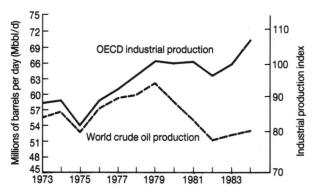

Figure 12.1   Oil production and economic growth, 1973–84

measures, it was likely that the gap between industrial production and oil production would continue to widen during the 1980s, especially in view of the long time lag between oil price stimulus and effect in terms of conservation.

The above analysis points to a gradual downward trend in oil production during the 1980s. How does the potential supply match up with this demand picture? Clearly, oil demand must equal supply in the medium and longer term as there is limited storage around the world compared with demand, and in any case most of the existing storage was already heavily used. Figure 12.2 shows how total oil production (already graphed in Figure 12.1) was split between OPEC and non-OPEC countries. Before 1973 the low price of oil meant that it was only economic to produce it in low-cost wells — and this meant OPEC wells in the majority. As the price of oil leapt from 1973 onwards many other exploration areas became viable (for example, the North Sea) and so non-OPEC oil production increased more rapidly. Since total world oil production was falling in the 1980s and non-OPEC production was rising, the share of oil production accounted for by OPEC was falling rapidly: it fell from half in 1979 to a third in 1984. Clearly, this sort of fall could not continue. When the world trade cycle was rising (as in 1982–4) the consequent rise in oil consumption allowed a steadying of OPEC's oil production. However, cyclical downturns in the world economy (for instance, from 1979 to 1982) reduced considerably the amount of oil that OPEC could sell, given that OPEC was keen to support the price and that the only way of achieving that was to restrict production. Non-OPEC producers sold all they could produce since they constituted the industrialized nations who would benefit if oil prices had to fall.

So by 1984 the OPEC countries only operated their oil fields at around 50 per cent of capacity, and this was having a major effect on nations whose main source of income was oil. As the oil price had risen from 1973, OPEC had spent the windfall profits on substantial new building and modernization. This created a call on capital inflows for some years ahead. However, by 1984, despite crisis cuts, OPEC was in a difficult position, as Figure 12.3 illustrates. Its current account surplus, which had soared following the two oil prices rises in the 1970s, had suddenly disappeared, and it was clear that its price leadership and the consequent loss of market share could not continue for much longer.

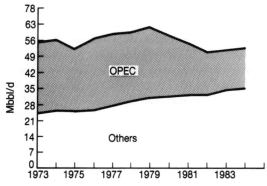

Figure 12.2 World crude oil production, 1973–84

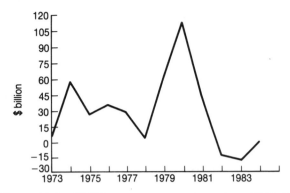

Figure 12.3 OPEC current account surplus, 1973–84

In these circumstances OPEC was likely to reduce prices under competitive pressure. The remaining question was when this would happen. As we have seen, OPEC loses market share most quickly in a cyclical downturn, so the most likely time for the oil price to fall back would be as downturn emerged. The next downturn was due around 1986, so that was the most likely timing of a break in the oil price.

12.4.2 The effect of the step change on ICI

The next matter of interest to ICI was the extent of the likely fall in oil prices. Here it was possible to be helpful but not precise. The oil price in the early 1980s was just above $30 per barrel. A small price fall would not stimulate demand a great deal, especially since oil demand responds to price changes very slowly. Neither would a small price fall discourage non-OPEC producers from producing all they could. It therefore seemed likely that the oil price fall would be considerable: a halving of the price was quite possible.

Because of this forecast, the heavy oil users within ICI were ready for action when the price fall started in January 1986. The initial fall was from $30 to $25 per barrel. At this stage (and perhaps it would have been even better done earlier), it was decided to investigate the effect of various possible price falls on the key performance indicators of ICI's vulnerable products. Three scenarios were investigated: in scenario 1, the price of oil falls to $22.50 per barrel; in scenario 2, it falls to $20 per barrel; and in scenario 3, it falls to $15 per barrel. The aim was to forecast the effect on product sales volumes, prices, margins and profits. Raw material (oil) prices were designated in dollars, selling prices in Deutschmarks (since the main market was western Europe), and the profit and margin forecasts were required in sterling. This necessitated a forecast of the effect of falling oil prices on exchange rates as well as the effect on product volumes, margins and so on. The method used was to estimate the effect of changing oil prices on the product volumes and margins using very simple econometric models, and then to use these relationships to drive a company planning model such as that described in Chapter 18. This will derive performance indicators such as profits.

At first glance it may appear that a 50 per cent fall in oil prices will have twice the effect of a 25 per cent fall. However, analysis of past data shows that this is not the case. In particular, the effect of a large fall in oil prices seems to have one effect in the short term and the opposite effect in the long term. It is important to set up econometric models ·-in such a way that differences in short-term and long-term effects can be estimated. In this exercise, the main effects were found to be as follows.

In scenario 1, compared with the $25 base case, sterling could be expected to weaken against the Deutschmark since Britain has significant oil production in the North Sea and a fall in the price of oil will weaken the balance of payments and therefore weaken sterling compared with non-oil currencies.

Since the price of the primary raw material was falling, an immediate increase in product margins would take place, leading to greater profitability. However, over a period of three months, some 80 per cent of this increased margin would be eroded due to competition in the marketplace. This conclusion was drawn from an analysis of past history.

Product sales volumes would increase slightly due to the fall in price arising from the margin movements analyzed above. Again the extent of this slight increase was estimated by a suitable regression model.

Product stock held by the company would decrease in value since its price would decrease as shown above. Stock losses could therefore be expected to reduce profits in the short term.

The net effect, when estimated by the company planning model, was to cause a slight increase in profit.

Scenario 2 found that the effects of the $20 oil price case would be similar to the $22.50 case, except that movements in exchange rates, profits and so on would be more marked.

According to scenario 3, there would be heavy downward pressure on the value of sterling. The effects on product performance indicators would be double the effects in scenario 2 with the following exceptions.

First, and apparently perversely, short-term sales volumes would probably fall dramatically. This is because customers would anticipate lower-priced materials in the future, and would be willing to run down stocks in the meantime to cover their commitments. This would be followed by a substantial rise in volume triggered by the substantial fall in price.

There would be higher UK inflation, and the possibility of a world debt crisis as the weaker oil producers failed to cope with a halving of the oil price.

Scenario 3 therefore splits into two possibilities: if the debt crisis fails to materialize then profits, margins and volumes will rise substantially in the longer term, although in the short term profits will suffer due to the buyers' strike and stock losses; if the debt crisis takes place then a deep recession is likely which will have adverse effects on product performance.

In view of the results of this model, contingency plans can be put in place to allow for any of the scenarios taking place. For example, stocks should be reduced to minimize stock losses, but should be sufficient to cope with the increased demand likely once prices have fallen. The fall in sterling should lead to the UK becoming a more attractive place to site product plants. And if a debt crisis materializes heavy stock reduction should be started in order to cope with lower demand. Sales to the poorer oil producing countries can expect to be hit particularly hard. The scenario approach therefore concentrates the mind on a small number of possible outcomes, and suggests suitable contingency plans to cope with any eventuality.

In the event, the oil price descended rapidly to $10 before stabilizing at around $15. A debt crisis did not ensue, so the increased product profits allowed the sector to enjoy a happy end to the 1980s.

CHAPTER 13

Long-term forecasting 4
Regression assumptions

13.1 Introduction

The data used for forecasting purposes often have strange properties which can affect the results of the analyses carried out. As mentioned in Chapter 12, empirical investigations of a range of techniques have shown that widths of theoretical confidence intervals for forecasts often underestimate the true widths by a factor of 3 or 4. For this reason we need to be very careful when using statistical techniques, both in parameter estimation and in the estimation of confidence limits. However, the difficulties involved should not mean that we never use statistical techniques for forecasting; just that we should proceed carefully, seeking, where necessary, the advice of a professional statistician. It can be highly dangerous to make use of the increasingly available standard statistical routines on PCs to obtain quick forecasts without reference to the potential problems involved. (The presence of such problems does, however, increase the value of good deterministic techniques, such as demographic analysis.)

Since regression analysis is a widely used technique in long-term forecasting, we shall now examine some of the assumptions made in carrying out such an analysis.

13.2 Heteroscedasticity

Regression assumes that the residuals about the fitted line are of constant variance. It is very common for this assumption to be broken: this leads to insecure parameter estimation. If the residuals are of constant variance then we have a situation of *homoscedasticity*, and if we have a non-constant variance then we have *heteroscedasticity*. An example of heteroscedasticity is shown in Figure 13.1, in which the residuals about the fitted straight line are increasing as x increases.

A typical situation of this type might arise when y represents sales and x is time. Sales are growing as time goes on, and the variability about the sales trend may well be a constant percentage of that sales trend. This means that the absolute value of the variability grows as time increases.

The possible responses to this situation are twofold. First, we could deflate the y series.

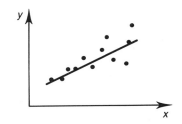

Figure 13.1   Heteroscedastic data

For example, if y represents the turnover at a given time x, then we can expect y to increase as x increases due to an inflationary environment, even if sales volume is constant. We would therefore deflate the turnover by retail prices (or some other suitable price series such as producer prices) to obtain an estimate of sales volume. This would give us the turnover at constant prices.

Second, we could transform the data. The most common transformation, particularly in econometric models, is the logarithmic transformation, where we take the logarithm of each data point y. This has the advantage of reducing the situation where residuals are a constant percentage of the data trend to homoscedasticity. However, sometimes this transformation is either too light (for example, an increasing variance remains increasing even after the transformation has been applied), or too severe (it over-corrects the situation). In these circumstances we can use the square root transformation $\sqrt{y}$ (a gentle transformation), or a reciprocal transformation $1/y$ (a more potent transformation).

It is a good idea to try all three transformations, plotting the residuals in each case, in order to decide which is the best one to use.

13.3   Serial correlation

Serial correlation is another very common problem in time-series analysis. In this case the residuals from the fitted model have runs of overestimates and underestimates. This is often a problem if cyclical movements have not been identified in the model. Figure 13.2 shows an example.

This creates a problem because one of the regression assumptions is that residuals should

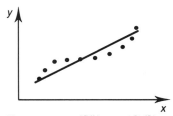

Figure 13.2   Serial correlation

be independently and identically distributed. In a model with serial correlation an underestimate at time t is likely to be followed by another underestimate at time $t+1$. This means that the residuals are not independent of one another.

The possible causes of serial correlation include the following:

1. A variable has been omitted. For example, we could have modelled new car registrations as a function of personal income and price. If serial correlation occurs with this model then perhaps we should include age as another variable. Alternatively, the model may not be identifying the trade-cycle effect in new car registrations, and this therefore needs to be included either explicitly or implicitly.
2. An incorrect functional form has been used. For example, a linear model may have been used where a nonlinear one is appropriate. This is a common failing of long-term models, especially if we are trying to model the life cycle curve for a product.
3. Outliers may be present. Strikes and similar disturbances give rise to outliers in data series. Fitting a model to such data can cause problems with parameter estimation. For example, Figure 13.3 shows how the fitted line attempts to compensate for a single outlier whereas the true line should go through all points except the outlier. The result is clear serial correlation.

The effects of serial correlation can be severe. First of all, the estimated confidence limits will be too narrow. Serial correlation may well account for a significant proportion of instances of underestimation of confidence interval width reported in the empirical studies mentioned at the beginning of this chapter. Related to this problem is the fact that t and F tests used to assess the statistical significance of the parameters estimated will give optimistic results. Finally, the variability of the parameters will be underestimated — we will get the impression that model parameters are well defined in the presence of serial correlation, when in fact they are not.

We have already dealt with the main test for serial correlation. This is the Durbin—Watson test described in Chapter 3.

There are a number of possible remedies for serial correlation. Experience will increase the certainty with which we choose the right remedy for a particular situation.

1. We should look for omitted variables. This is a common situation and is known as improving the model specification.
2. We should look to see if the wrong type of underlying trend has been used, and/or if there are outliers in the data. Outliers can be omitted or corrected for, and the analysis

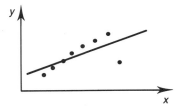

Figure 13.3 An outlier causing serial correlation

performed again. We should examine any assumptions we make about the linearity of the underlying trend. It may well help to detrend the data by using percentage changes or differences of successive data points. However, this can lead to a deterioration in the model fit.

3. If neither of the first two remedies is appropriate, then we should fit an autoregressive model to the residuals or include an autoregressive term in the original model.

4. An alternative to remedy 3 is to use generalized least squares, a technique developed specifically for this eventuality. However, the complexities of this technique create problems of their own, and its value is not always self-evident.

13.4   Dealing with serial correlation: an example

Fabuloid Holdings has interests in a consumer good, the sales of which need to be forecast. This product is sold entirely into the US market, and so a regression approach is attempted, using personal disposable income as the independent variable. The data are shown in Table 13.1.

The estimated regression line is given by the equation

$$Y = -1573 + 42.15X_1$$

Table 13.1   Fabuloid sales, disposable income and unemployment

Year	Fabuloid sales Y	Disposable income X_1	Unemployment (%) X_2
1955	9921	273.4	4.4
1956	10 668	291.3	4.1
1957	10 803	306.9	4.3
1958	11 163	317.1	6.8
1959	12 108	336.1	5.5
1960	12 402	349.4	5.5
1961	12 804	362.9	6.7
1962	13 734	383.9	5.5
1963	15 279	402.8	5.7
1964	17 148	437.0	5.2
1965	19 071	472.2	4.5
1966	20 307	510.4	3.8
1967	21 888	544.4	3.8
1968	24 534	588.1	3.6
1969	26 532	630.4	3.5
1970	27 753	685.9	4.9
1971	30 018	742.8	5.9
1972	33 600	801.3	5.6
1973	37 500	903.1	4.9
1974	39 303	983.6	5.6
1975	40 920	1076.7	8.5

which explains 99.0% of the variability in Y. As with so many regression solutions, this seems too good to be true, and indeed it is. First, the fit is as high as it is mainly because both variables increase with time. A similarly impressive result would have been obtained had the independent variable been the number of births in Africa! However, a second important problem can be found with the analysis. The Durbin–Watson statistic is 0.63. The tabulated lower and upper limits for a sample of 20 and one independent variable at a significance level of 0.01 are 0.95 and 1.15, respectively. Since 0.63 is less than the lower limit, positive serial correlation is indicated.

Following the suggested remedies for serial correlation given above, we could estimate a regression line using year-on-year percentage changes for sales and disposable income instead of the original variables Y and X_1. We can call these two new variables X_3 and X_4, respectively. The effect of this is to eliminate the trend effect which was the first objection to the original regression run. The estimated regression equation becomes

$$X_3 = 1.440 + 0.815X_4$$

which now explains only 22.9 per cent of the variation in the new dependent variable X_3. This is a typical result of detrending the data, and is a better reflection of the forecasting power of the equation. The Durbin–Watson statistic is now 1.305, and this is above the upper limit of the tabulated values. Therefore serial correlation is no longer a problem. However, the single explanatory variable considered does not provide an adequate forecast: a much higher proportion of the variability needs to be explained. We might therefore add another explanatory variable — this would be X_5, the year-on-year percentage change in unemployment (the original variable being X_2 as given in Table 13.1). The new equation becomes

$$X_3 = 2.669 + 0.705X_4 - 0.080X_5$$

This equation has two statistically significant X variables, accounts for 48.6% of the variation and provides a Durbin–Watson statistic of 1.84 — a further improvement on the already satisfactory level achieved in the previous regression. Although about half of the variation is still unaccounted for, the analyst should stop at this point since a good rule of thumb is to have only one regressor for every ten points of data. An equation of this form accounting for half of the variation is quite good, although of course to provide a sales forecast we need to have forecasts of disposable income and unemployment. This introduces a further element of uncertainty into the forecast.

13.5 Multicollinearity

Estimation difficulties occur when the independent variables are highly correlated. This is the problem of *multicollinearity*. The estimated regression coefficients can be highly misleading, as the following example shows.

Suppose we are trying to predict sales of a consumer good by regressing it on family income and family size. The correlation matrix arising from our data set may be as follows:

	Sales	Income	Size
Sales	1.00	0.88	0.74
Income		1.00	0.87
Size			1.00

The estimated regression equation might well be

Sales $= 3.52 + 2.28 \times$ Income $- 0.41 \times$ Size

In this case we can note the following points:

1. Both income and size correlate well with sales (from the correlation matrix). The correlation coefficients are 0.88 and 0.74.
2. However, income and size are themselves highly correlated (0.87).
3. As a result of this collinearity, the regression coefficient for size has a negative sign despite the clear positive correlation between sales and size.
4. The value of R^2 for this data set is 0.785 (that is, 78.5 per cent of the total variance is explained by the two variables). However, a regression of sales on income alone would have given an R^2 of 0.781. There is very little to be gained in adding the size variable to the equation despite its high correlation with sales. This is because most of the information that size provides is already given by the income variable. We would therefore use the regression of sales on income alone to provide forecasts.

The problems arising from multicollinearity are as follows:

1. As we have seen in the example, a positive sign in a one-variable regression can change to a negative sign when a second variable is introduced.
2. Estimates of the regression coefficients are highly variable from sample to sample. In other words, the confidence limits on the regression coefficients tend to be very wide.
3. It is difficult to separate the effects of the variables. In the above example, is it income or size which is causing changes in sales?

Possible solutions to these problems are the following:

1. Gather more data to reduce the internal correlations — that is, deliberately choose data which create low internal correlations and omit data which create high internal correlations.
2. Select fewer variables (as in the above case). It is not uncommon for the non-statistician to choose too many explanatory variables on the basis that we do not want to miss out any potentially useful variable. Unfortunately, multicollinearity — either in its obvious form as above, or in a disguised form when no single internal correlation appears to be too high but the combination of correlations causes problems — becomes more and more of a problem as the number of variables increases. It is worth remembering that simple is usually best, and that in any case we should not exceed one variable for every ten data points.
3. Use ridge regression (see Chapter 14).
4. Use stepwise regression (see Chapter 14).

Long-term forecasting 5

Regression topics

14.1   Introduction

In Chapter 13 we identified two useful techniques for overcoming regression problems such as multicollinearity. These are ridge regression and stepwise regression. We now describe these two techniques very briefly, and then go on to discuss some other points which need to be noted when employing multiple regression on time-series data.

14.2   Ridge regression

In order to understand ridge regression fully, an advanced statistical text must be consulted (see, for example, Draper and Smith 1981). However, this book aims to consider business applications rather than heavy statistical theory, so only an outline of what ridge regression attempts to do will be given. Some knowledge of matrix algebra and multiple regression is assumed, and if the following discourse is beyond the reader then he/she is strongly advised to consult a statistician rather than to attempt any analysis unaided.

In multiple linear regression, the estimation of the regression coefficients β is achieved by the equation

$$\hat{\beta} = (X^TX)^{-1} X^Ty$$

where $\hat{\beta}$ is an m × 1 vector, X an n × m matrix and y an n × 1 vector, defined respectively as follows:

$$\beta = \begin{bmatrix} \hat{\beta}_1 \\ \hat{\beta}_2 \\ . \\ . \\ . \\ . \\ . \\ \hat{\beta}_m \end{bmatrix}$$

$$X = \begin{bmatrix} x_{11} - \bar{x}_1 & x_{12} - \bar{x}_2 & & x_{1m} - \bar{x}_m \\ x_{21} - \bar{x}_1 & x_{22} - \bar{x}_2 & \cdots & x_{2m} - \bar{x}_m \\ \cdot & \cdot & & \cdot \\ \cdot & \cdot & & \cdot \\ \cdot & \cdot & & \cdot \\ x_{n1} - \bar{x}_1 & x_{n2} - \bar{x}_2 & \cdots & x_{nm} - \bar{x}_m \end{bmatrix}$$

$$y = \begin{bmatrix} y_1 - \bar{y} \\ y_2 - \bar{y} \\ \cdot \\ \cdot \\ \cdot \\ \cdot \\ \cdot \\ y_n - \bar{y} \end{bmatrix}$$

and the equation to be fitted is

$$y = \hat{\beta}_0 + \hat{\beta}_1 x_1 + \hat{\beta}_2 x_2 + \ldots + \hat{\beta}_m x_m$$

If multicollinearity is a problem then the matrix $X^T X$ will be very nearly singular and its inverse $(X^T X)^{-1}$ unstable. For this reason the regression coefficients $\hat{\beta}$ are subject to a high degree of variation. Ridge regression attempts to overcome this problem by changing $X^T X$ so that it is not nearly singular. Instead of inverting $X^T X$, we invert $X^T X + kI$ where k is a positive number and I is the identity matrix. That is, we define

$$\hat{\beta} = (X^T X + kI)^{-1} X^T y \quad k > 0$$

Clearly, when $k=0$ we have the classical multiple linear regression situation with its problem of multicollinearity, and as we slowly increase k the matrix $X^T X + kI$ becomes less and less difficult to invert, thus lessening the problem of multicollinearity and obtaining better estimates of β. However, we are also moving further and further away from the original data set and so what we really need is to consider the smallest possible value of k which gives reasonably stable estimates of the regression coefficients.

It is normal to plot a graph of the regression coefficients against the value of k. It is then fairly easy to identify when the regression coefficients have converged. For example, in Figure 14.1 the rapid changes in the coefficients below $k = k_1$ indicate a region of

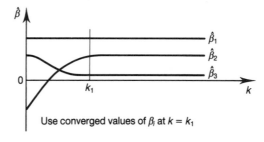

Figure 14.1   Ridge regression plot

high multicollinearity, whereas the estimated coefficients are relatively stable for $k >$ k_1. In this case we would use the regression coefficients estimated with $k = k_1$. Unfortunately, sometimes one or more of the regression coefficients refuse to converge, and in this case the expert help of a statistician is required.

14.3 Stepwise regression

Clearly one of the main problems in multiple regression which can lead to multicollinearity is the number of variables considered. We require a regression equation using a subset of the available variables which explains a large proportion of the total variability while introducing as little multicollinearity as possible. We can build up this list of variables by using stepwise regression.

This technique involves carrying out a sequence of regressions. Beginning with the null case — a regression on no independent variables — add significant variables one by one until there is no significant variable to add. Next, delete insignificant variables one by one until there is no further insignificant variable to delete. Continue adding and deleting until convergence is achieved. The problem of multicollinearity means that the order of variables added at one stage is not necessarily the reverse of the order of variables deleted in the next stage. Similarly, a variable once added can easily become insignificant and therefore be deleted due to the effect of a second variable added later. It is not generally true, therefore, that no deletion stage is necessary.

A statistic known as the *partial F*-statistic is used to test the significance of candidate variables in both the addition and deletion phases of the procedure. This compares the sum of squares accounted for using a $(k+1)$-variable regression as opposed to a k-variable regression. it is defined as

$$\text{Partial } F = \frac{SS_{k+1} - SS_k}{(SS_{\text{total}} - SS_{k+1})/(n-k-1)}$$

where n is the total number of data points, SS_{total} is the total sum of squares and SS_k is the sum of squares accounted for by the k-variable regression.

Variables are added in order of maximum significance, and are deleted in order of minimum significance. The partial F-statistics are calculated at each stage for each candidate variable, and they may well change significantly from run to run. Often the significance of a candidate variable will increase after the addition of another variable, as in the following example. Most computer packages which offer stepwise regression will allow you to specify the critical values of the partial F-statistic: these can be different depending on whether you are adding or deleting variables.

For example, suppose we have 30 observations, and six candidate variables which we can use. Note that it is inadvisable to use all six variables, since our rule of thumb, indicating a maximum number of variables equal to the number of observations divided by 10, would imply a maximum of three variables in this case. The first stage involves adding variables as long as they are significant. Table 14.1 shows the results of this exercise.

Note that (assuming a normal critical value of 4 for the partial F-statistic) variables 2

Table 14.1   Stepwise regression report

Variables entered	Residual degrees of freedom	R^2	Partial F
None	29	0	—
3	28	0.6368	49.09
2,3	27	0.8784	63.27
2,3,6	26	0.8805	0.18

and 3 are accepted, but variable 6 is rejected as its partial F-value is less than 4. Note also that although variable 3 has the highest partial F at the first stage, once that variable has been added, variable 2 has an even higher F-statistic. This stage of the stepwise regression procedure therefore ends with only variables 2 and 3 in the equation. We would then proceed on to the deletion stage in which we would attempt to drop either variable 2 or 3. Clearly, variable 2 cannot be deleted since it has just been introduced with a significant partial F, but variable 3 may have a low partial F at this stage if variables 2 and 3 are highly correlated. The significance of variable 3 when it was entered indicates that it is likely to remain significant, however. The stepwise regression procedure would test this assumption by calculating the relevant partial Fs and deleting variables if necessary.

14.4 Overfitting

When we are carrying out a multiple linear regression, the fit will improve each time we add another variable. It is very tempting to add more and more variables until a 'desirable' level of fit is obtained. When analyzing time series in this manner it is not difficult to find a considerable number of variables which apparently correlate significantly with the dependent variable. However, a superior level of fit does not necessarily imply a superior forecasting equation. This phenomenon of adding too many variables is known as *overfitting*.

As a very simple example, suppose we have six data points and we fit five variables. Then whatever the variables are (as long as they are independent) we shall obtain a perfect fit. The equation is highly likely to be useless from the point of view of forecasting, however! Another way of looking at this problem is that if a second data set is analyzed then the regression coefficients in the multiple linear regression are likely to be very different from the first analysis if overfitting has occurred.

To test for overfitting the following procedure is appropriate. First, fit the multiple regression equation to the data set and calculate the mean square error. Then, use the fitted equation to 'predict' the dependent variable using a second data set. Again, calculate the MSE. If the second MSE is much higher than the first then overfitting has probably occurred. Often a second data set is not available. In this case we need to assess the out-of-sample fit using part of the data set. For example, if we have 20 years of sales data, we could fit a multiple linear regression to the first 15 points and assess the model's performance over the final five points of the original data set. A marked difference between the in-sample MSE and the out-of-sample equivalent implies that overfitting may have occurred.

Clearly we need to restrict the number of variables so that overfitting does not occur. A useful rule of thumb, already mentioned, is to allow only one variable for every ten observations. The stepwise regression procedure helps to guard against overfitting by calculating partial F ratios rather than straight correlation coefficients, and therefore will not allow the inclusion of variables whose explanatory power is equivalent to that of a combination of the variables already included. However, even stepwise regression is not immune to overfitting, and the above tests need to be applied in cases of doubt.

14.5 Lagged variables

It can be quite useful to consider lagged variables in many forecasting applications. For example, the sales of a consumer good may depend on interest rates ahead of the sales period, rather than at the same time. Similarly, advertising may have a delayed effect, and this would imply the use of a lagged variable.

If y_t is sales at time t, x_{t-1} is the value of an independent variable at time $t-1$ and z_{t-3} is the value of variable z at time $t-3$, then we could fit the model

$$y_t = a + bx_{t-1} + cz_{t-3}$$

In general, we can also include a lagged version of the dependent variable of the right-hand side as follows:

$$y_{t+1} = a + bx_{t-1} + cy_t$$

In all cases a, b and c are the fitted regression coefficients.

We can find the best lag to use by using the auto- or cross-correlation function. By correlating sales (y) with an independent variable (x) for various lags we obtain a graph such as that shown as Figure 14.2. The lag giving the maximum value of the correlation coefficient is the optimum lag to use.

We should only include the lagged variable if the correlation coefficient is statistically significant. Two problems arise in the use of lagged variables. First, the correlation coefficient that we are testing in Figure 14.2 is the *maximum* correlation obtained for any lag. This means that significance is only achieved at a higher correlation than would be

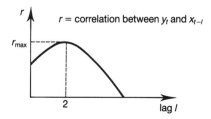

Figure 14.2 The cross-correlation function and optimum lag

the case if we were only taking one random lag and testing that. In other words, if we test the maximum correlation then we are likely to include more lagged variables than we should in our model. This is a difficult problem since the correlation coefficients for adjacent lags in Figure 14.2 are clearly highly correlated, and so a simple adjustment for the number of lags tested is not possible.

The second problem involves the regression of a variable on a lagged version of itself. If we want this sort of model we must allow for the fact that the normal Durbin—Watson statistic will be biased upwards and thus no longer valid. Fortunately, the Durbin—Watson h statistic is available for use in these circumstances. However, we will not concern ourselves with it here.

14.6   Dummy variables

Dummy variables, which can only take the values 0 and 1, can be very useful in forecasting. For example, suppose we are forecasting sales (y) as a function of the income of the buyer's family (x_1). It is possible that males and females may act differently, and so we introduce a dummy variable (x_2) which takes the value 0 for males and 1 for females. Our data may be as follows:

y	x_1	x_2
7.2	26.2	0
8.4	23.7	1
3.7	27.1	1
5.2	24.2	0
1.7	28.3	1
.	.	.
.	.	.
.	.	.

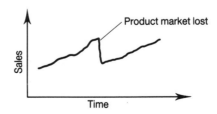

Figure 14.3   Discontinuous sales data

We can now fit a model of the form

$$y = a + bx_1 + cx_2$$

from which we can deduce the different buying patterns of males and females as well as the effect of income.

A second use of dummy variables in time-series data is when a discontinuity occurs in the sales series. Figure 14.3 shows a typical sales graph in which one of the company's products has been discontinued. By including a dummy variable which takes the value 0 before the discontinuity and 1 afterwards, we can examine the effects of other variables after accounting for the discontinuity.

CHAPTER 15

Long-term forecasting 6
Correlation analysis

15.1 Introduction

In previous chapters we have discussed some of the difficulties in using regression analysis
for forecasting time-series data. Unfortunately, we have really only scratched the surface
— there are many more problems involved in carrying out regression analysis even using
just one explanatory variable. This single-variable regression analysis is often dubbed
correlation analysis. The problems arise mainly because of the normal traits of economic
data such as their susceptibility to trade-cycle fluctuations, and correlation analysis is often
used with scant regard to the extent of the forecasting errors which are often unexpectedly
introduced.

15.2 Correlation analysis

Correlation analysis in business parlance consists of the prediction of one variable (for
example, sales growth) using a forecast of another explanatory variable (such as growth
of the industrial production index). We use past data on both of these two variables to
fit a straight-line relationship between them. This relationship can be used to convert next
year's prediction for IPI growth into a forecast of sales growth. Figure 15.1 shows how
a simple regression equation

Sales growth (% p.a.) = $a + b \times$ IPI growth (% p.a.)

is fitted to data and then predictions of IPI growth of 1 per cent for the next year and
3 per cent for the year after can be converted into sales-growth forecasts of 1.8 per cent
and 3.6 per cent. Indeed, this method can be used to provide forecasts of sales growth
for the next few years individually, or to assess the likely average growth rate for sales
over the next 5 years, say, based on the forecast trend growth rate for the IPI over that
period.

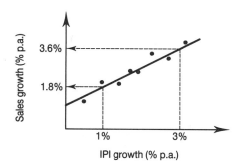

Figure 15.1   Correlation analysis

15.3   Errors in historical IPI data

We are all aware that predictions of this nature may not work out in practice because the relationship which was followed in the past did not continue into the future. However, there is another possible explanation. This involves errors in the historical IPI data used to construct the regression line. In Chapter 4 we discussed the problem of rebasing and revision of production indices. Unfortunately, these features of production indices lead to substantial errors in the fitted regression line.

We obviously want to use the most up-to-date data in order to construct our regression line. But the more up-to-date the data are, the more susceptible to revision they are. Only when the data are more than about 10 years old are they proof against substantial revision. We therefore have to ask ourselves what will be the effect of variability in the x (explanatory) variable. If the practical effect is small then perhaps we can ignore it. If it creates substantial bias in the regression line then we have a problem.

Suppose we have a perfect predictor (x) of the growth rate of sales (y). Assuming that there is no residual error, then the data will lie perfectly along the fitted line as in Figure 15.2, and as long as we can forecast x accurately we have a powerful tool to predict y. Let us assume that the forecast equation is $y = x$.

Let us now assume that the revision error for the x-variable varies from -1 per cent to $+1$ per cent. Now the data will be spread out in the x-direction and a simple regression

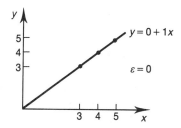

Figure 15.2   No revision error in x-variable

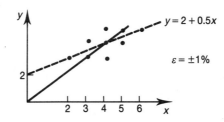

Figure 15.3   Revision error of ± 1%

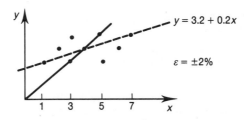

Figure 15.4   Revision error of ± 2%

would fit the line $y = 2 + 0.5x$. This assumed revision error is relatively modest by practical standards for production data and yet the slope of the line has been reduced by no less than 50 per cent. This is illustrated in Figure 15.3, which shows the correct line as a solid line and the fitted line as a broken line.

If we allow the revision error to increase to ± 2 per cent then the fitted regression line will become $y = 3.2 + 0.2x$. The slope of the line is now only 20 per cent of the true value! This situation is shown as Figure 15.4.

Revision errors therefore can cause major estimation problems with the regression line. However, the above example also shows that revision errors cause substantial bias in the slope of the line. In the presence of revision errors the expected slope of the line *will always be too small*. We cannot ignore revision errors in the *x*-variable and assume that the errors will be small and unbiased — both of these assumptions are invalid. If this conclusion is true of simple regression (correlation analysis) it is equally true of multiple regression analysis, where some of the explanatory variables are subject to revision. Many econometric analyses suffer from this major problem.

15.4   Product maturity effects

Correlation analysis fits a single straight line to a data set. The assumption is that the underlying model is time-invariant — in other words, the line does not move up or down as time goes on. If we are analyzing a mature product's sales then this is probably a reasonable assumption. However, most products are not mature, and, over the span of time to which the historical data refer, the trend growth rate of the product is probably falling as in Figure 15.5.

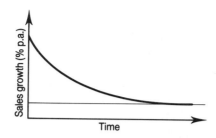

Figure 15.5 Trend growth rate of a maturing product

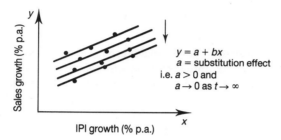

Figure 15.6 Descending regression line as time proceeds

Therefore the expected growth rate for this product in the early stages of its history will be higher (at a given level of general economic activity) than later on in its life cycle. The correlation analysis model should take this into account by allowing the line to fall gradually as time proceeds. This is easily illustrated as in Figure 15.6, but is much more difficult to model statistically. All too often it is assumed that the line remains stable through time, and the fitted line therefore overestimates forecast sales growth in the future.

When carrying out any sort of correlation analysis using a non-mature product (and this includes the more complicated case of econometric models), it is sensible to plot the graph of the historical data as a directed graph so that the time trend can be seen clearly. The model should therefore be

Sales growth $= a + b \times$ IPI growth $+ f(t)$

where $f(t)$ describes the time trend in the data, and tends to zero as t tends to infinity. In practice, $f(t)$ can be modelled by fitting a trend curve to the data before carrying out the correlation analysis.

15.5 Lagged responses

Another common problem area for the practitioner of correlation analysis is when product sales react to a move in the economy after a time lag, or indeed when product sales lead the economy. This is illustrated in Figure 15.7. The correct model to fit in this case is

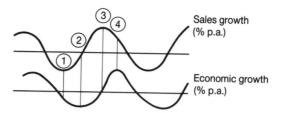

Figure 15.7   Sales lead economic activity

Sales growth $(t) = a + b \times$ IPI growth $(t+c)$

where c can be positive or negative.

The normal correlation analysis graph would respond to this situation by forming a closed loop (see Figure 15.8). Clearly, fitting a normal regression line without taking into account the lead or lag will provide a less than accurate forecast. It is therefore important to test for significant leads or lags by using the cross-correlation function before carrying out a suitable regression analysis. (Cross-correlation calculates the correlation between two series when one of the series is lagged by a given number of time periods.)

Combining this problem with the problem of product maturity would give a directed graph of the form shown in Figure 15.9. It is clearly valuable to draw a directed graph of correlation analysis data before carrying out any analysis.

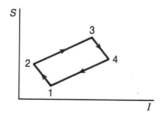

Figure 15.8   Directed graph of lagging data

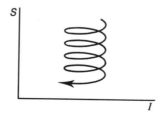

Figure 15.9   Directed graph of lagging data with maturing product

15.6 Nonlinearity

Correlation analysis assumes that there is a linear relationship between sales growth and economic growth. Unfortunately, this assumption is often unreasonable in times of extreme economic activity. A company will often respond to very high economic activity by panic buying, fearful of running out of stock. The sales growth under these circumstances will be higher than would be implied by a straight-line model. Conversely, in extremely adverse economic conditions companies will often stop ordering altogether in a desperate attempt to keep stock levels under control. Again this leads to a deviation from a straight-line model, as shown in Figure 15.10.

There is little that can be done to forecast the extent of sales growth or decline under extreme economic conditions — such conditions occur infrequently and even the sparse data available are often inconsistent.

15.7 Aliasing trade cycle and long-term trend

One of the major pitfalls of correlation analysis is the confusion or aliasing between the effect of the trade cycle and the long-term trend. Suppose, for example, we have fitted a line as in Figure 15.11. The mean point is where sales growth (S) is 5 per cent and IPI growth (I) is 3 per cent. However, the slope is greater than 1, so that the predicted

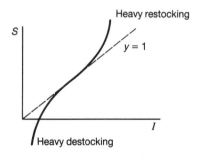

Figure 15.10 Nonlinearity in extreme economic conditions

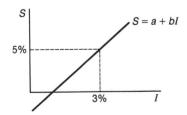

Figure 15.11 Correlation analysis with slope greater than 1

sales growth for small IPI growth rates is negative. Are we really predicting a sales decline for an increase in IPI?

The answer to this question depends on whether the small value of IPI growth is a new average growth rate over the course of a trade cycle or whether it is the IPI performance at the bottom of a trade cycle. In the first scenario, I averages 3 per cent p.a. over the course of a cycle, and an I-value of 0.5 per cent p.a. (say) represents a bad year within such a cycle. In the second, the average growth rate of the economy may have fallen to 0.5 per cent p.a., within a spread over the cycle of (say) -2 per cent to $+3$ percent.

The historic data have been collected under the assumption that the average value of I is 3 per cent p.a. over a trade cycle, so the prediction is only really valid for the same average growth rate of the economy. The line describes what happens to sales as the economy moves up and down from its 3 percent equilibrium position. In other words, the line predicts what will happen over the course of a trade cycle where I averages 3 per cent p.a.

The slope of the line is greater than 1 because of the pipeline effect, where the effect of a cyclical swing of the economy is amplified up the chain of suppliers for a particular end-use (as discussed in Chapter 7). It is entirely possible that in such circumstances sales growth will be very low when the economy turns down, and will rise spectacularly when the economy sees above average growth. However, over the course of a complete trade cycle the average growth of sales will be equal to the growth in the economy plus some constant (a) which allows for the extra growth derived from substitution of competing materials. In this case the constant a is 2 per cent (5 per cent $-$ 3 per cent).

If the *average* growth rate of the economy declines to 0.5 per cent p.a. (say) it is not reasonable that the average growth in sales will turn negative as implied by the line. It is much more likely that average sales growth will be the economic growth (0.5 per cent) plus the 2 per cent substitution growth rate: 2.5 per cent in all. The line is therefore only valid as long as average growth remains the same as it was in the historic data period. As soon as this average economic growth changes, we need to split the graph into a trend line which is calculated using our estimate of substitution growth and which will have a slope of 1, and cycle lines which describe the movement of sales growth over the course of a cycle with a given average IPI growth rate. This is illustrated in Figure 15.12.

Substitution is a relative price effect (that is, it depends largely on the price of the product, or indeed the quality of the product, against that of competitive materials). It is not related

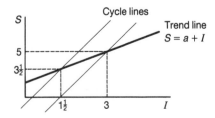

Figure 15.12 Trend lines and cycle lines

to economic growth rate. For this reason the substitution effect is a constant 2 per cent in the above example and does not decline with economic growth.

15.8   Aliasing long-term trend and long economic cycles

Just as the trend and trade cycle can be aliased or confused, so can trend be aliased with longer economic cycles. Figure 15.13 shows the 18-year construction cycle plotted schematically against the growth rate for a product (such as PVC) used heavily in the building industry. The PVC line is indicative of its performance in an average western European market. Around 1970 PVC growth was high, on average, over the course of a trade cycle, due to the high position of the construction cycle. Similarly, PVC growth reflected the rapid fall in the construction cycle in the 1970s to reach a very low value around 1980, before rising somewhat in the 1980s as the construction cycle recovered. Correlation analysis carried out in 1970 would have indicated high PVC growth whatever the growth rate of the economy (see Figure 15.13).

The same analysis carried out in 1980 would have seen a much lower regression line, and would have predicted very low PVC growth through the 1980s, thereby underestimating the true outcome. To indicate the extent of the dangers in forgetting about the effects of longer cycles, consider two forecasts for western European PVC growth carried out in 1970 and 1980. The 1970 forecast used the upper line in Figure 15.13 and assumed a continuation of IPI growth of 3.5 per cent p.a. on average. PVC growth was forecast at more than 10 per cent p.a. By 1980 the lower line was being used and IPI growth was assumed to be 1 per cent p.a. This implied a zero-growth scenario for PVC in the years ahead! The first forecast would have suggested building new plant to satisfy demand (which did not materialize) and the second forecast would have written PVC off too soon. The danger in 1990 is in thinking the PVC has got a second wind, and ignoring the severe construction downturn likely in the early and mid-1990s.

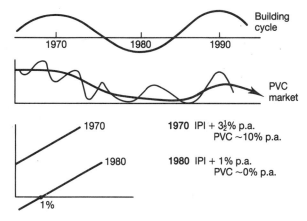

Figure 15.13 Correlation analysis for PVC in 1970 and 1980

The truth is that PVC trend growth was about 6 per cent p.a. in 1970, declining to 4.5 per cent in 1980 and 4 per cent in 1990 for a constant 3 per cent p.a. IPI growth. On top of these figures we need to superimpose growth or decline on behalf of the construction industry.

CHAPTER 16

New product models

So far we have considered a number of methods of producing sales-volume and market forecasts. These methods all require products which have passed the early stages of development, and therefore possess historical data of reasonable length. We need to forecast the markets for such products in order to support planning decisions about, for example, the advisability and timing of new capital investment.

However, not all products are mature. We often need to forecast a market which has little or no history. For example, our company's Research Department may have developed a promising new product. We need to decide whether to support this product with capital investment. Is it worth spending money on new plant and earmarking working capital in order to develop the product from the research phase to the production phase? A decision of this sort will involve forecasting sales volume, margins and cash requirements — all without the backcloth of much (if any) historical data. All too often the decision as to whether to support a new product is based on little analytical forecasting and much wishful thinking. It is important to recognize the tools we have available to provide analytical forecasts where data are scarce. Often even an 'honest' expert view assumes no downside risks and proves highly optimistic. Such forecasts are revised downwards in successive time periods to provide the well-known 'herring-bone effect' (Figure 16.1).

In this chapter we look at some of the ways we can make analytical forecasts in these circumstances. We shall cover both the case of no data and that of little data. The new-product problem illustrated above is an example of a case with no data. If the product is launched using a pilot plant, a second decision point may be reached after 3—4 years: do we spend a lot of money uprating the pilot plant to a full-scale plant? At this stage 3—4 years' history has been obtained — insufficient to drive the models discussed in previous chapters. This is an example of a case with little data. Alternatively, we may have a new product which we could launch into a market which a competitor has already entered. If the competitor has been selling its product for 4 years (say) then we can use market intelligence to provide us with estimates of the market for those 4 years — again we have a case with little data (despite the fact that we are thinking of entering the market with no sales history of our own).

Of course, we should not expect extreme accuracy from a forecast made without the benefit of a substantial run of data. On the other hand, typical new-product forecasting

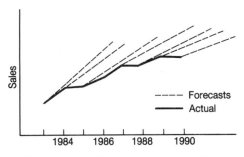

Figure 16.1 The herring-bone effect

models augment scarce and often erratic data with 'hidden data' describing how the product market can be expected to develop, based on the experience of other products. By using such models we can often avoid pitfalls such as bias which tend to be a feature of opinion-based forecasts.

16.1 Data-free methods

As an example we shall use the case of a high-performance plastic developed by our Research Department. It has good temperature and stress properties — significantly better than those of the material traditionally used in the construction of commercial aircraft. This area is seen as the major potential application of the plastic. It is proposed that we build a pilot plant. Should we go ahead?

To answer this question we need answers to the following questions:

1. Is the cash available to build a pilot plant?
2. If the pilot plant is successful, would the cash be available to expand production facilities later?
3. Would the new product fit sensibly into our existing product portfolio?
4. What competitive reaction is likely from:
    (i) the supplier of the traditional material;
    (ii) other possible producers of the new plastic?
5. What margins can we expect, taking a long-term view?
6. What sales volume are we likely to see?

Questions 1 and 2 are easily answered. Question 3 is best answered by portfolio analysis — for example, the Boston matrix or one of the other matrix methods (see, for example, Abell and Hammond 1979). It depends on cash and profit forecasts which require margin and volume projections. Questions 4 and 5 are linked in that the competitive supplier may well fight back by lowering prices in the short to medium term, but will probably not deviate significantly from the experience curve in the long term (see Chapter 17). Our product will probably make a loss in the first few years anyway, and this loss will be accentuated by the above competitive reaction. On the other hand, low prices may well deter other potential producers of the new plastic from entering the market. A view of the timing of the entry of competitive producers is probably best obtained through market intelligence, however, together with an analysis of the strategies and cash and/or profit pressures of those competitors. We will not concentrate on margin forecasts or cash-flow forecasts here — these are covered in Chapters 17 and 18. Instead, we shall consider Question 6: how to forecast sales volume.

16.1.1   End-use analysis

A number of potential end-uses will have been suggested for the product. Each one needs to be followed up. In each case we must be sure that the new product has significant advantages over the existing product employed in that end-use, and that the relative costs of the two materials are such that profits can be made in the longer term by the new product. If these conditions are satisfied then we can develop a forecast for the use of our new product in this application. This is done by proceeding as follows:

1. Forecast the market for the end-use. In our example this involves forecasting the sales of commercial aircraft, probably by means of existing expert forecasts by trade bodies.
2. Forecast the penetration or market share of our product into the end-use market. This will depend at least partly on pricing policy, and is an inexact science. However, an idea of how quickly new materials are integrated into an industry can be gained by looking at the introduction of innovative materials into that industry in the past.
3. Apply the formula:

    Forecast sales = forecast market × forecast penetration

   This exercise can be repeated for all the major end-uses, and the results summed to give a sales forecast for the product as a whole. Figure 16.2 illustrates this procedure

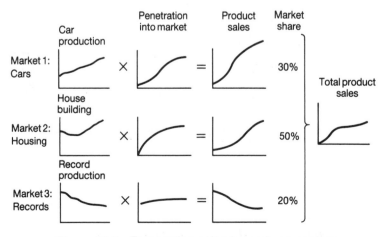

Figure 16.2   Forecasting sales by end-use analysis

for a product with three main end-uses accounting for 30, 50 and 20 per cent of total sales, respectively.

Unfortunately, this method suffers from the problems of providing a penetration forecast and the problem of foreseeing new end-uses in future years. On the other hand, no historical data are required and the method encourages a logical thought process as opposed to wishful thinking.

16.1.2 Product parallels

The *product parallels* method is also independent of past sales data, and ensures that sales forecasts are at least in line with past experience. A shortlist of similar products with a similar spread of end-uses is drawn up. The market for these products in their early years is examined. The annual market growth rate for each product is calculated: this should be done from the end of the development phase, since before that stage the market tends to grow in fits and starts. This is repeated for all the similar products. The average growth experience for these products can then be used to provide a post-development growth projection for the new product (see Tables 16.1 and 16.2).

This method constrains the market forecast to be in line with past experience, and requires no data on the new product (except for a post-development starting point for market size). The answers need to be cross-checked against end-use analysis to ensure that the longer-term market size is reasonable.

This method can prove suprisingly accurate, although it obviously requires a sensible choice of parallel products and a sensible estimate of when their development phase ended. Because new product growth tends to be high, we can ignore economic effects in the data history: a recessionary year usually has a relatively small effect on high-growth products. Again there could be effects due to changing selling prices of the products, but at this stage of a product life cycle sales volume is fairly price-insensitive — in any case the price early in the product history is likely to be well above that of competitive materials. It

Table 16.1 Historical data on two products

| | Product 1 | | | Product 2 | | | |
	Year	Market	Growth % p.a.	Year	Market	Growth % p.a.	Average growth
Development	1972	0.1		1979	2.0		
phase	1973	1.0	900	1980	10.0	400	650.0
	1974	9.3	830	1981	23.0	130	480.0
Post-development	1975	21.7	133.3	1982	51.2	122.6	128.0
phase	1976	40.2	85.3	1983	79.3	54.9	70.1
	1977	61.7	53.5	1984	115.6	45.8	49.6
	1978	69.9	13.3	1985	146.3	26.6	20.0
	1979	88.4	26.5	1986	182.0	24.4	25.4
	1980	103.6	17.2	1987	216.0	19.2	18.2

Table 16.2 Forecast for new product

		New product		
	Year	Market	Growth % p.a.	
Development phase	1987	0.7		
	1988	3.0		History
	1989	11.4		
Post-development phase	1990	26.0	128.1	
	1991	44.2	70.0	
	1992	66.1	49.5	Forecast
	1993	79.4	20.1	
	1994	99.5	25.3	
	1995	117.6	18.2	

is only as the product matures and unit costs decline as market share increases that volume will become price-sensitive.

16.1.3 Customer research

As another cross-check, potential *customers* can be asked how they see the markets for a new product with the properties and prices you propose. The advantages of this approach are that it acts as a counterbalance to any tendency you may have towards wishful thinking, and that new markets, which you may not have foreseen, could be anticipated by the customer who has the benefit of a forecast of his/her industry's technological future.

16.2 Models requiring historical data

16.2.1 Market life cycles

Products can be split into three types:

1. *Non-repurchasable products*. Such products 'never' wear out or become outmoded (Figure 16.3). A wedding ring is an example, although the market potential would increase as time progresses in this case.
2. *Replacement-purchase products*. These products wear out and replacement items are required after a time lag (Figure 16.4). Per-capita consumption is limited. Toasters are an example.
3. *Repurchasable products*. The per-capita consumption of these products is relatively unconstrained. Repeat purchases are made, and the time lag before these repeat purchases start is fairly small (Figure 16.5). Many industrial products fall into this category.

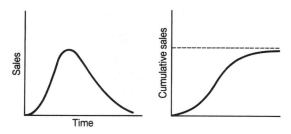

Figure 16.3   Non-repurchasable product

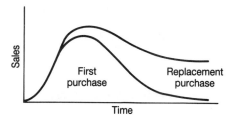

Figure 16.4   Replacement-purchase product

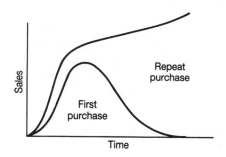

Figure 16.5   Repurchasable product

The models we shall consider estimate the profile of first purchases. As such they are ideally suited to type 1 products, very good for type 2 products over a fair number of years, and useful for type 3 products in providing a 'lower limit' forecast in the early years of market development. In the industrial sector these models can be used directly to provide a lower limit for the early years, or they can be used to analyze end-uses which may be typified by type 2 products.

16.2.2 Concave diffusion models

A diffusion process describes how sales of a new product diffuse through the 'population' of potential adopters. These models are analogous to the spread of an epidemic through a population. The diffusion model should describe the sales life cycle curve for first purchases of a product based on a parsimonious set of parameters. These parameters will be estimated initially by analogy with the past history of similar products. After a few years it is possible to estimate the model parameters from the new product data set itself. The simplest representation is the *concave diffusion model* (see Fourt and Woodlock, 1960).

The concave diffusion model assumes that sales in time period t are proportional to the previously untapped market. The model is

$$Q_t = r\bar{Q}(1-r)^{t-1}$$

where Q_t is sales at time t, $\bar{Q}$ is potential sales, and r the rate of penetration of untapped potential.

The model is completely specified by the two parameters r and $\bar{Q}$. At time zero the untapped market is $\bar{Q}$, so the sales volume in period 1 is $r\bar{Q}$. At time 1 the untapped market has fallen to $\bar{Q} - r\bar{Q} = \bar{Q}(1-r)$, so the sales volume in period 2 is $r\bar{Q}(1-r)$. At time 2 the untapped market is $\bar{Q}(1-r) - r\bar{Q}(1-r) = \bar{Q}(1-r)^2$, so sales volume in period 3 is $r\bar{Q}(1-r)^2$. Clearly, sales volume in period n will be $r\bar{Q}(1-r)^{n-1}$ (see Figure 16.6). Substituting $r = 0.3$ and $\bar{Q} = 0.4$, we have

$$
\begin{aligned}
Q_1 &= r\bar{Q} &&= 0.3 &&\times 0.4 &&= 0.12 \\
Q_2 &= r\bar{Q}(1-r) &&= 0.12 &&\times 0.7 &&= 0.084 \\
Q_3 &= r\bar{Q}(1-r)^2 &&= 0.084 &&\times 0.7 &&= 0.059
\end{aligned}
$$

This curve produces declining sales through time. Initially market research would evaluate r and $\bar{Q}$. After two periods, r can be re-estimated by calculating the ratio of the second period's sales to the first period's sales. In our example

$$1 - r = \frac{0.084}{0.12} = 0.7$$

so $r = 0.3$ as expected. Successive re-estimates of r would be averaged unless the environment changes (for instance, if more marketing effort were applied, or if a new price policy were adopted), in which case the latest calculation of r would be used without averaging previous estimates. The model can easily be adopted for a product with a gradually increasing asymptote. If $\bar{Q}_t$ is the asymptote at time t, then

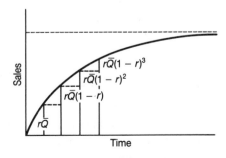

Figure 16.6 Simple concave diffusion model

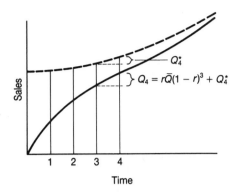

Figure 16.7 Advanced concave diffusion model

$$Q_t^* = \bar{Q}_t - \bar{Q}_{t-1}$$

is the increase in asymptote between time $t-1$ and time t. So sales at time t are given by

$$Q_t = r\bar{Q}(1-r)^{t-1} + Q_t^*$$

(see Figure 16.7).

To take an extended example, a new book is being launched in 1988. We are hoping for sales of 3000, with 30% of the remaining market covered each year. In other words, $\bar{Q} = 3000$ and $r = 0.3$. These figures reflect previous experience with similar books. Our pre-launch forecast is therefore

$$
\begin{aligned}
Q_1 &= r\bar{Q} & &= 0.3 \times 3000 & &= 900 \\
Q_2 &= r\bar{Q}(1-r) & &= 0.3 \times 3000 \times 0.7 & &= 630 \\
Q_3 &= r\bar{Q}(1-r)^2 & &= 0.3 \times 3000 \times 0.49 & &= 441 \\
Q_4 &= r\bar{Q}(1-r)^3 & &= 0.3 \times 3000 \times 0.343 & &= 309
\end{aligned}
$$

Our sales forecast at this stage is

Year	Sales volume	Cumulative sales
1988	900	900
1989	630	1530
1990	441	1971
1991	309	2280

At the end of 1988 sales have reached 1120. We can now update our forecast. We can assume that our estimated market size of 3000 is correct, or that our penetration rate of 30 per cent is right. We would normally modify our estimate of market size and retain our initial value of r. We can update our estimated value of $\bar{Q}$ by solving

$$Q_1 = r\bar{Q}$$
$$1120 = 0.3\bar{Q}$$
$$\therefore \quad \bar{Q} = 3733$$

Our amended sales volume forecast would be calculated as before, but with the new higher ceiling:

Year	Sales volume	Cumulative sales
1988	1120	1120
1989	784	1904
1990	549	2453
1991	384	2837

After another year's data we have two equations in two unknowns. Suppose that 1989 sales are 890, giving cumulative sales of 2010. Then

$$Q_1 = r\bar{Q} \qquad = 1120$$
$$Q_2 = r\bar{Q}(1-r) = \quad 890$$

Dividing the second equation by the first we obtain

$$1 - r = 0.7946$$
$$\therefore \quad r = 0.2054$$

and substituting into the equation for Q_1

$$\bar{Q} = 5454$$

Now our forecast becomes

Year	Sales volume	Cumulative sales
1988	1120	1120
1989	890	2010
1990	707	2717
1991	562	3279

Another year's data gives us three equations in two unknowns which can therefore be estimated by the method described above for the last two years. Nonlinear optimization could be used, but is more complicated, although it would simultaneously re-estimate $\bar{Q}$. As a third alternative, both r and $\bar{Q}$ can be re-estimated by applying the procedure used for the first two years' data on years 2 and 3. This has the disadvantage that it discards the information provided by year 1's data. Suppose that 1990 sales are 630. Then

$$Q_1 = r\bar{Q} \qquad = 1120$$
$$Q_2 = r\bar{Q}(1-r) = \quad 890$$
$$Q_3 = r\bar{Q}(1-r)^2 = \quad 630$$

Using the simple method (the first of the three methods outlined above) our new estimate of r is

$$1 - r = \frac{630}{980} = 0.7079$$

$$\therefore \quad r = 0.2921$$

Averaging this estimate of r with the previous one (0.2054) we obtain a new estimate of 0.2488. Our new forecast would therefore be as follows:

Year	Sales volume	Cumulative sales
1988	1120	1120
1989	890	2010
1990	630	2640
1991	473	3113
1992	356	3469

For example, sales volume for 1991 would be estimated as

$$630 \times (1 - r) = 630 \times 0.7512 = 473$$

Clearly if the estimate of $\bar{Q}$ were of particular importance, we would have to use a nonlinear fitting routine, or solve for r and $\bar{Q}$ using only the data for 1989 and 1990.

16.2.3   S-curve diffusion models

Concave diffusion models are suitable for products with immediate appeal, backed up with massive marketing and advertising effort. If the market takes longer to accept a new product, then sales will *rise* in the early years. In terms of the speed of their reaction to any new product, customers can be categorized as follows:

1. Innovators: These customers desire to be different.
2. Early adopters: These are opinion leaders who quickly recognize the product's value.
3. Early majority: These are deliberate in their buying patterns, but adopt new products earlier than average.
4. Late majority: These are sceptical, adopting the product only after majority opinion has legitimized it.
5. Laggards: These are the traditional and suspicious customers, who will only buy the product when it has assumed a measure of tradition.

Rogers (1962) analyzed and discussed these categories. He found that new adopters could be pictured as shown in Figure 16.8. Cumulative sales would follow an S-curve (Figure 16.9).

The form of the curve in Figure 16.8 invites characterization by the normal curve. However, early attempts to describe actual sales data by a normal curve met with mixed

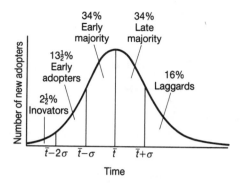

Figure 16.8 Succession of new adopters

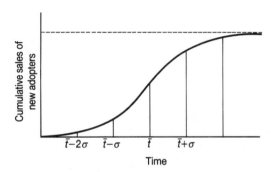

Figure 16.9 Cumulative sales profile

success. The lognormal curve was suggested as a more logical choice, and although it tends to fit better than the normal curve, other studies show that the logistic curve performs better still. All three curves follow the characteristic *S*-shape.

The logistic curve is usually modelled as

$$\ln\left(\frac{Q_T}{\bar{Q} - Q_T}\right) = a + bt$$

where Q_T is cumulative sales to time t, ln denotes logarithms to base e, and a and b are constants to be estimated.

More recently the gompertz curve has been seen as more generally applicable: this curve is not restricted to having a point of inflection exactly half way to its asymptote.

16.2.4   Epidemiological diffusion models: the Bass model

The Bass model is an epidemiological diffusion model. It assumes that a new market develops like an infection. Non-adopters of the product may be influenced either by

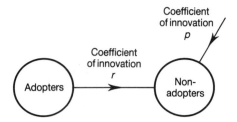

Figure 16.10   The epidemiological defusion process

advertising, or by companies which have already adopted the product. The probability that a non-adopter will adopt the product this year depends on the coefficient of innovation (advertising) and on the coefficient of imitation (the influence of adopters) — see Figure 16.10.

Clearly the number of adopters is zero at time zero so p is all-important then. After a reasonable time r becomes dominant as the number of adopters rises.

The Bass model is

$$Q_t = \left(p + r\frac{Q_T}{\bar{Q}}\right)(\bar{Q} - Q_T)$$

where Q_t is the number of new adopters in period t, Q_T the cumulative number of adopters to period t, $\bar{Q}$ the potential number of adopters, r the effect of each adopter on each non-adopter, and p the individual conversion rate in the absence of the adopter's influence. The first bracketed term increases with time whereas the second bracket decreases. This gives an S-shaped curve when integrated. For a successful new product it is normal to expect r to be greater than p (Figure 16.11).

Estimation of the Bass model

The Bass equation can be rewritten as

$$Q_t = p\bar{Q} + (r - p)Q_T - \frac{r}{\bar{Q}}Q_T^2$$

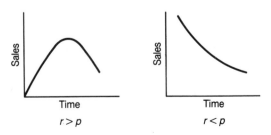

Figure 16.11   New buyer sales curve

that is, as a second-order equation in Q_T. This is simply

$$Q_T = a + bQ_T + cQ_T^2$$

where $a = p\bar{Q}$, b $= r - p$, $c = -r/\bar{Q}$. These parameters can be estimated as soon as 3 years' data are available (or 2 years if $\bar{Q}$ is assumed). Parameters can be updated in successive years thereafter. At each stage we can calculate the estimated peak sales level

$$Q_{t*} = \bar{Q}(p + r)^2/4r$$

and the predicted timing of this peak

$$t^* = (1/(p + r)) \ln(r/p)$$

In practice we can model Q_t as a function of Q_{T-1} to allow forecasts to be made more easily.

We conclude this chapter with an example. The market for UK video recorders is as shown in Table 16.3. We use the model (with S_t denoting sales at time t)

$$S_t + p\bar{S} + (r - p)S_{T-1} - (r/\bar{S})S_{T-1}^2$$

Taking all nine points, regression of S_t on S_{T-1} gives

$$S_t = 0.910 + 0.9053S_{T-1} - 0.000\,249\,7S_{T-1}^2$$

Solving for p, r and $\bar{S}$, we obtain $r = 0.9056$, $p = 0.0003$, $\bar{S} = 3627$. This implies a total market of 3.6 million before replacements, second purchases and so on. If this value is thought to be unrealistic, the exercise could be repeated with a constrained value for $\bar{S}$.

A peak of 900,000 sales can be expected in 1984 (using the formulae given earlier in Section 16.2.4).

The low value of p implies that heavy advertising is unlikely to have a major effect (exemplified by the slow sales growth in the early years).

Table 16.3 UK market for video recorders (thousands)

Year	Sales S_t	Cumulative sales S_T	S_T^2
1972	1	1	1
1973	3	4	16
1974	6	10	100
1975	10	20	400
1976	15.9	35.9	1 288.8
1977	23.2	59.1	3 492.8
1978	67.6	126.7	16 052.9
1979	106.9	233.6	54 569.0
1980	199.5	433.1	187 575.6

CHAPTER 17

Price and margin forecasting

17.1 Introduction

So far we have only considered the forecasting of volume series such as product sales volume. This sort of forecast is of great importance to the business world. However, no business likes to exist without a profit forecast, and so over the next couple of chapters we will investigate how to develop price and margin forecasts, because price forecasts are vital in building up profit forecasts. This chapter therefore deals with price and margin forecasts, and the next describes how we can use a company planning model to derive profit forecasts.

17.2 Prices and margins

It will repay us to have a clear idea of the concept of *gross margin* before we start. The description below is not strictly accurate but is close enough (except for accountants!). Gross margin is the difference between sales value and raw material costs (more strictly this is value added). Thus if we buy 5 tonnes of naphtha at a total cost of £1000 and convert it into polyethylene which we sell for £2500, then our gross margin is £1500.

More usually, we quote gross margin per tonne of output — this is called unit gross margin (UGM, or gross margin per tonne). In the above example we bought naphtha at £200 per tonne and sold polyethylene at £500 per tonne. The UGM is therefore £300 per tonne.

If selling prices rise while raw materials prices remain constant, then UGM will rise. Similarly, if raw material prices fall whilst selling prices remain constant then the UGM will rise. Obviously the reverse events will lead to an erosion in UGM.

A sudden rise in raw materials prices will often have a two-phase effect on margins. At first margins will be squeezed or reduced because of unchanged product prices and increased raw materials prices. However, the industry will not be willing to suffer sharply lower profitability, and usually selling prices are adjusted upwards over a period, often of a few weeks, so that the UGM is the same as before the raw materials price rise. Competition in the marketplace may cause some reduction in UGM, but this reduction

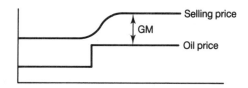

Figure 17.1   Gross margins under the influence of rising raw materials prices

is usually relatively small. Figure 17.1 illustrates the situation for a petrochemical producer whose raw material is oil.

There is usually therefore a short period of squeezed margins when raw materials prices rise, but in the medium and longer term UGMs are relatively steady. Since UGMs are more consistent than prices, we tend to analyze UGMs rather than prices, and translate to price forecasts by making assumptions about the future level of raw materials prices. So how do we forecast UGMs?

17.3   Experience curves

In the 1960s the Boston Consulting Group showed that in many industries manufacturing costs (after adjusting for inflation) fall at a constant rate for each doubling of cumulative production. In other words, the manufacturing costs involved in producing 1 tonne of product fall by a constant percentage from 100 tonnes of cumulative production to 200 tonnes, and the same percentage from 200 tonnes to 400 tonnes and so on. Prices also decline at the same sort of rate as shown in Figure 17.2, giving rise to a constant profit margin per tonne assuming that costs include the cost of wages and so on. Figure 17.2 is clearly indicative only: real data will show all sorts of short-term variation. In addition, the constant profit margin will not apply in the very early years of the product history. It must also be borne in mind that this graph refers to costs for the industry as a whole, not for an individual company.

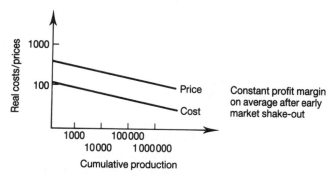

Figure 17.2   The Boston Experience Curve and real prices

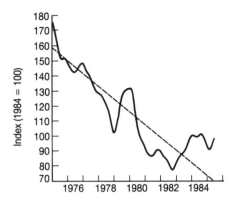

Figure 17.3 A typical real unit gross margin plot

Since the cost per tonne is falling and profit per tonne is constant, and since part of 'cost' is depreciation and wage costs, then UGM must be falling since gross margin is depreciation plus wage costs plus profit. Plotting real unit gross margin (RUGM) against time will often give a linear graph in the long term. An example of a petrochemical product is shown in Figure 17.3.

The general method for forecasting gross margins and prices is therefore as follows. Plot RUGM. If this is roughly linear, then fit a regression line. Multiply by forecast inflation figures to give a UGM forecast. Multiply by forecast volume to give a total gross margin forecast. Use a company planning model (see Chapter 18) to convert gross margins into prices. This analysis should be carried out in the units of the main trading country. For example, western European petrochemicals are traded in Deutschmarks so we need to use Deutschmarks as our currency and German inflation figures to deflate, even if our main operations are in some other European country.

The above procedure gives a long-term forecast for margins and prices. However, there are plenty of shorter-term deviations, as can be seen from Figure 17.3. In particular, there are cyclical changes as margins are squeezed in the trough of a trade cycle and expand as business conditions improve. We shall consider this medium-term problem next.

17.4 The price−volume lag

Margins and prices are affected by the trade cycle. In general, we can expect them to show a cyclical variation around the long-term declining trend in UGMs. This is illustrated in Figure 17.4.

Remembering the trade-cycle clock (Chapter 7), we saw that prices tend to rise and fall some 9 months after volume on average. If a forecast of cyclical changes in volume is available then it can be used to provide a cyclical forecast or prices and margins. The lag for a particular product may not be the average 9 months: we need to estimate the lag by using cross-correlation analysis on historical volume and price data. We can do

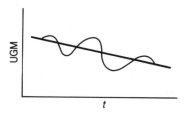

Figure 17.4   Cyclical profile of unit gross margins

Figure 17.5   Price—volume relationship

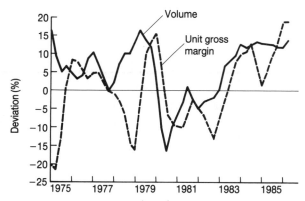

Figure 17.6   Company X volume and unit gross margins in Deutschmarks: deviations from trend

this by varying the lag until we obtain the highest correlation. Figure 17.5 illustrates how we would hope to forecast cyclical price movements from cyclical changes in volume.

Figure 17.6 shows how such a relationship works out in practice. There is clearly a fair amount of variability, but the lagged relationship is fairly obvious. We also need to bear in mind that the lag also suffers from variability — sometimes it is as low as 3 months and sometimes as high as 15 months. We can also see that the amplitude of the cyclical volume swing corresponds well with the amplitude of the margin swing. Thus we can make a sensible forecast of both the timing and the amplitude of cyclical margin swings around the long-term trend.

17.5 Price hysteresis

Prices are dictated to some extent by the occupacity of the plant. (Occupacity is the percentage of the plant's capacity being used.) In other words, if the plant is working flat out (at 100 per cent occupacity) then prices are likely to be extremely firm. On the other hand, if it is only working at 80 per cent occupacity (80 per cent of its maximum rate) then prices are likely to be somewhat lower. Clearly, during the course of a trade cycle, occupacity will swing from low to high and back to low again (assuming that no extra plant has been built during this period).

However, the upswing in prices which the rise in occupacity implies is by no means linear. As occupacity rises, prices rise slowly until the plant is working nearly flat out, at which point prices rise more steeply as shortages emerge. But prices do not retrace their steps as occupacity falls again. At first prices only fall slowly from their peak levels, and it is not until occupacity reaches some critical value (often around 70 per cent for industrial goods) that prices collapse, as shown in Figure 17.7. The next upswing proceeds gradually as prices rise slowly until occupacity approaches 100 per cent again when a surge in prices is seen.

In some ways the explanation for this phenomenon (known as *price hysteresis*) is simple. As we have seen, changes in price follow some 9 months behind changes in volume. Since

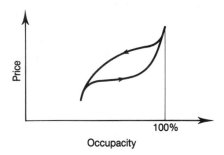

Figure 17.7 Price hysteresis

Table 17.1 A typical occupacity–price relationship

Quarter	Occupacity (%)	Price
1	98	120
2	95	119
3	78	118
4	70	82
5	80	82
6	90	85
7	95	87
8	97	119

volume is proportional to occupacity, it is natural that changes in occupacity should lead changes in price. This is what the hysteresis effect demonstrates.

As an example, consider a product whose occupacity and price over a number of quarters are shown in Table 17.1. The collapse in price only started when occupacity had declined below 78 per cent, and the sharp recovery in price had to wait until occupacity was above 95 per cent.

CHAPTER 18

A company planning model

18.1 Introduction

Companies need to forecast in order to plan effectively. It is common for a 'planning cycle' ↲ to take place once a year. In this planning cycle, a detailed forecast might be made of the company's business for the next year, and an indicative forecast provided for the following 2 years. These forecasts will include projections of the company's volume, prices, margins, turnover, cash flow and profit, and will be drawn up under various assumptions about how the economy will proceed over that 3-year period.

This forecast can be used as a 'planning model' in order to investigate how changes in the basic economic and company assumptions will affect the key performance parameters for the business. We are therefore concerned with a scenario model which relates the linkages between the main company variables. This model can then be used to test whether it is prudent, for example, to spend a certain amount on capital expenditure in the medium term, or whether the proposed spending will lead to unacceptable pressures on the company if the economic assumptions turn out to be too optimistic.

In this chapter we will examine a typical company planning model which links together the key performance indicators and allows scenario forecasting and planning to take place. The model uses a highly simplified version of the company accounts and would tend to be run by the company's planning department rather than its accounts department.

18.2 The structure of the model

The model would be driven by a number of different elements. First, we need to take account of environmental forecasts. Such forecasts would involve exchange rates, industrial activity, raw material costs and so on. In most cases these data will be provided by the economics department of a large company, or will have been abstracted from the forecasts of one of the organizations providing projections of the business environment, be they international organizations (the OECD or IMF) or national bodies (the London Business School, NIESR, Treasury, Bank of England).

Second, we would need forecasts of the company's sales volume, unit gross margins, wage and salary costs and depreciation. The first two of these have been covered earlier in this book; wage costs relate to human resource assumptions, and depreciation depends on capital spending plans. In general, volume and margin forecasts will be subject to far greater error than the wage and depreciation projections.

We then need to construct a 'what-if' model which uses the above forecasts to generate projections for turnover, price and profit. The model can be run under various assumptions on the environmental variables and forecast variables. This will lead to a range of possible profit pictures for the future which may lead to a reassessment of spending plans. The model can then be rerun with the new spending plans, leading to new volume and margin projections, and new profits derived. The process is illustrated in Figure 18.1.

18.3   Key accountancy relationships

In order to understand the working of the model, some key but highly simplified accountancy relationships need to be mentioned. The first of these defines *turnover*:

Turnover = Raw material costs + Gross margin

More strictly, 'gross margin' should be termed 'value added', but for the simplified planning

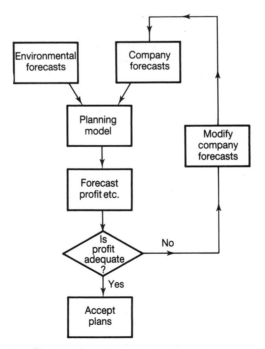

Figure 18.1   Iterative planning model process

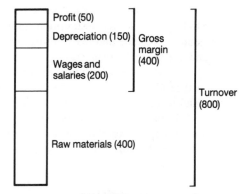

Figure 18.2 Split of turnover

model described here the two terms are roughly interchangeable since we are primarily concerned with trends rather than absolute values of the margins.

The second relationship breaks down *gross margin*:

Gross margin = Wages/salaries + Depreciation + Profit

Figure 18.2 shows how a typical industrial company with a turnover of £800m would deliver a profit of £50m.

Finally, given fixed costs (FC), variable costs (VC), gross margin (GM) and turnover (TO), we can state an equation for total costs (TC):

$$TC = FC + VC$$

where

$$VC = TO - GM$$

since

$$TO = FC + VC + \text{Profit}$$

These are simple accountancy definitions — for further explanation the reader is referred to a simple accountancy text (for example, Kohler 1970). However, it is worth noting here that it is in the area of variable costs that the difference between value added and gross margin becomes apparent. For example, where do we put advertising costs? However, for simplicity's sake and in order to concentrate on the workings of a planning model rather than becoming bogged down in accountancy terms, we will stay with the definitions already used.

18.4 Planning model flow diagram

Using the accountancy relationships described above, we can piece together a flow diagram for our planning model. Let us suppose that we are dealing with a UK petrochemical manufacturer whose only raw material is oil. (Again this is a simplification since other raw materials will doubtless also be involved.) The oil price is quoted in US dollars, so in order to convert oil price forecasts from dollars into pounds sterling, we also need a forecast of the dollar exchange rate. Under our simplified assumption that oil is the company's only raw material, the raw materials price index (RMPI) is proportional to the oil price in sterling.

Variable costs depend on the RMPI and on the volume forecast, although they will also depend on the mix of products and the efficiency of the plants. The volume and UGM forecasts will imply a gross margin forecast, and adding the gross margin forecast to the variable costs forecast we obtain a turnover forecast. Since price is turnover divided by volume, the turnover and volume forecasts imply a price forecast. By subtracting wages and salaries, depreciation and variable costs forecasts from the turnover forecast we finally obtain a profit forecast. The flow diagram which describes this process is shown in Figure 18.3.

18.5 Planning model spreadsheet

Clearly this sort of application is well suited to a computer spreadsheet. Figure 18.4 therefore shows such a spreadsheet. The first two quarters of the years are historical and we are forecasting the third and fourth. For planning-cycle work we would expand the spreadsheet 3 years into the future.

The calculations are different depending on whether one is in historical mode or forecast mode: both sets of calculations are shown in Figure 18.4. In historical mode we would

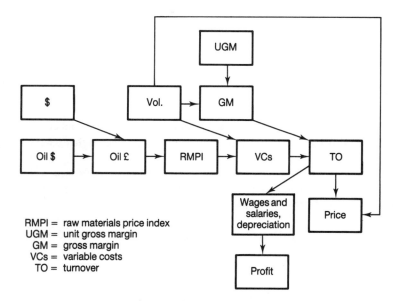

Figure 18.3 Planning model flow diagram

	HISTORY				FORECAST	
	Q1	Q2	Calculation ←	Calculation →	Q3	Q4
ENVIRONMENT						
$	1.90	1.85	a	a	1.80	1.80
Oil ($)	20	19	b	b	19	19
Oil (£)	10.53	10.27	$c = \frac{b}{a}$	$c = \frac{b}{a}$	10.56	10.56
VOLUME						
Vol (SA)	107.9	106.8	$d = \frac{f}{e} \times 100$	d	108	109
Seasonal factor	101	103	e	e	96	100
Vol	109	110	f	$f = d \times \frac{e}{100}$	103.7	109
MARGINS						
UGM (SA)	74.7	77.4	$g = \frac{i}{h} \times 100$	g	78	79
Seasonal factor	102	101	h	h	98	99
UGM	76.1	78.2	$i = \frac{g}{f} \times 100$	$i = g \times \frac{h}{100}$	76.4	78.2
VAR. COSTS						
RMPI	100	97.5	$j = c \times \frac{100}{10.53}$	$j = c \times \frac{100}{10.53}$	100.3	100.3
RMPI/VC	1.19	1.15	$k = \frac{j}{l}$	k	1.15	1.15
VC	84	85	$l = m - n$	$l = \frac{j}{k}$	87.2	87.2
ACCOUNTS						
TO	167	171	m	$m = n + l$	166.4	172.4
GM	83	86	n	$n = f \times \frac{i}{100}$	79.2	85.2
Depreciation	21	21	o	o	21	21
W + sales	42	44	p	p	44	44
Profit	20	21	$q = n - o - p$	$q = n - o - p$	14.2	20.2
Price index	153.2	155.5	$r = \frac{q}{f} \times 100$	$r = \frac{q}{f} \times 100$	160.5	158.2

Figure 18.4 Planning model spreadsheet

know the values of the exchange rate, oil price, volume, turnover, gross margin, depreciation, wages and salaries and profit. The other variables are calculated. For example

$$VC = TO - GM$$

$$UGM = GM/VOL$$

Certain scaling factors are used to give sensible values for the various indices. For example, the RMPI is the oil price times a multiplier which is calculated so that RMPI for the first quarter is 100.

In forecast mode, we have forecast assumptions for the dollar, oil price, volume, UGM, the ratio of RMPI to VC (including mix and efficiency effects), depreciation and wages and salaries. From these are derived the key performance indicators as described in Section 18.4.

This is clearly a simplified representation of the spreadsheets used in practice. For example, we would also calculate cash flow in order to facilitate capital spending assessments. If the 3-year profit profile looks weak under various environmental and company assumptions, then we would look for cost-cutting factors (such as lower capital spending or lower wage costs) in order to increase profits to a more acceptable level.

CHAPTER 19

Monitoring

19.1 Introduction

When we have developed a forecast we should not just forget about it. Forecasting is a difficult business and even the best forecasters get it wrong. It is therefore important to check whether the forecast matches the out-turn as time progresses. This process is known as *monitoring*. We need to monitor both short-term forecasts such as those of the production process for stock-control purposes, and longer-term forecasts such as business-planning forecasts. In the first case we need an automatic method that can be readily computerized since it will need to be carried out many times per day. On the other hand, longer-term forecasts often involve monthly or quarterly data and a manual method is often appropriate here, although it helps if the model is computerized.

In this chapter we will consider both types of method, as well as a further forecasting method which is closely linked with one of the monitoring models.

19.2 Trigg and Leach's forecasting method

We introduce a new forecasting method here because it leads naturally on to the first monitoring method. We have already discussed the method of exponential smoothing. This is a short-term method for stationary series. The formula is

$$\hat{y}_{t+1} = \alpha y_t + (1 - \alpha)\hat{y}_t \tag{19.1}$$

(see Section 5.1.3). We choose the value of α either as a standard value (for instance, 0.2) or as the value which minimizes the mean square error on an in-sample basis. However, it may well be that the best value of α to use differs according to the volatility of the data series. Thus it may be sensible to use a value of $\alpha = 0.1$ for the first part of the data, whereas a better value for the later data may be $\alpha = 0.3$. It would be nice to have a method which automatically adapts the value of α as we progress through the data to provide optimum forecasts taking into account the nature of the data at that point. Trigg and Leach's method allows this to be done.

With Trigg and Leach's method we have an adaptive value of α which we can call S_t.

S_t rises when the volatility of the series rises and falls when the data become more stable. The formula is the same as that for exponential smoothing (equation (19.1)), except that α is replaced by S_t:

$$\hat{y}_{t+1} = S_t y_t + (1 - S_t)\hat{y}_t \qquad (19.2)$$

The value of S_t is the ratio of the exponentially smoothed error (E_t) to the exponentially smoothed mean absolute deviation (M_t). The former is given by

$$E_t = \alpha e_t + (1 - \alpha)E_{t-1} \qquad (19.3)$$

where $e_t = y_t - \hat{y}_t$; the latter is given by

$$M_t = \alpha|e_t| + (1 - \alpha)M_{t-1} \qquad (19.4)$$

We can then write:

$$S_{t+1} = |E_t/M_t| \qquad (19.5)$$

Normally the system is allowed to settle down by constraining S_t to be 0.2 (say) for the first three or four points. α is commonly set equal to 0.2.

For example, weekly sales volume at Aromco for the last 11 weeks has been as follows:

135 140 160 150 130 140 140 145 160 155 165

What forecasts should we make using single exponential smoothing with an adaptive parameter (that is, Trigg and Leach's method)?

Let us set up the method as above, but we shall constrain the adaptive parameter to have a maximum value of 0.4. In other words, if S_t is calculated to be more than 0.4 then we shall call it 0.4. The table of calculations is set out in Table 19.1. Thus S_t is constrained to be 0.2 for the first four points, and thereafter is calculated according to the appropriate formula. α has been set to 0.2 for the calculations of E_t and M_t. As an example, the forecast for period 8 is

Table 19.1 Trigg and Leach analysis for Aromco data

Period	Data y_t	Forecast	Error e_t	E_t	M_t	S_t
1	135.00					0.20
2	140.00	135.00	5.00	1.00	1.00	0.20
3	160.00	136.00	24.00	5.60	5.60	0.20
4	150.00	140.80	9.20	6.32	6.32	0.20
5	130.00	142.64	−12.64	2.53	7.58	0.40
6	140.00	137.58	2.42	2.51	6.55	0.33
7	140.00	138.39	1.61	2.33	5.56	0.38
8	145.00	139.01	5.99	3.06	5.65	0.40
9	160.00	141.40	18.60	6.17	8.24	0.40
10	155.00	148.84	6.16	6.17	7.82	0.40
11	165.00	151.31	13.69	7.67	9.00	0.40
12		156.78				0.40

$$F_8 = S_7 Y_7 + (1 - S_7)F_7$$
$$= 0.38 \times 140 + 0.62 \times 138.39$$
$$= 139.01$$

where

$$S_7 = \text{ABS}(E_6/M_6)$$
$$= \text{ABS}(2.51/6.55)$$
$$= 0.38$$

with

$$E_6 = 0.2e_6 + 0.8E_5$$
$$= 0.2 \times 2.42 + 0.8 \times 2.53$$
$$= 2.51$$

and

$$M_6 = 0.2\text{ABS}(e_6) + 0.8M_5$$
$$= 0.2 \times 2.42 + 0.8 \times 7.58$$
$$= 6.55$$

Note that in this example, the adaptive parameter is often more than 0.4, so we reduce the value to 0.4 as this is seen as the highest practical value of use.

As a forecasting method Trigg–Leach has an intellectual appeal — we might expect that it would perform better than exponential smoothing. However, in practice it does not provide any major advantages over the simpler method (see, for instance, the forecasting competitions carried out in the 1980s, for example Makridakis *et al.* 1982). For this reason we would prefer the simpler technique for straight forecasting. However, Trigg–Leach's approach does lend itself to monitoring data, as we shall now see.

19.3 Trigg's tracking signal

The aim of this monitoring system is to detect when the forecast being used becomes inappropriate for the situation. It can be used to monitor *any* forecasting system. The formulae are very similar to those used in the Trigg–Leach forecasting method. E_t and M_t are defined exactly as in equations (19.3) and (19.4), but they are then related as follows:

$$S_t = E_t/M_t \tag{19.6}$$

Note that the formula for S_t does not involve an absolute value as is the case in Trigg–Leach's forecasting method (equation (19.5)).

S_t is the tracking signal, which varies between -1 and 1. Values close to the extremes may be significant. For example, at the 95% confidence level:

if $\alpha = 0.1$ then S_t is significant if $|S_t| > 0.42$;

if $\alpha = 0.2$ then S_t is significant if $|S_t| > 0.58$;

if $\alpha = 0.3$ then S_t is significant if $|S_t| > 0.71$.

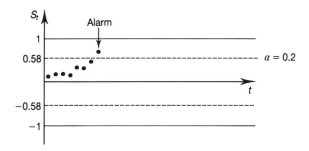

Figure 19.1   Trigg's tracking signal

A positive sign for S_t implies that forecasts are below the actual data, whereas a negative value of S_t implies that forecasts are above the actual data. The system has been found useful for quality control and sales forecasting applications.

In practice, a chart would be drawn up with alarm limits written in, and the forecast would be investigated if the alarm were sounded (that is, if S_t proved to be significant). Such a chart is shown in Figure 19.1. A significantly high value such as that shown in Figure 19.1 may suggest, for example, that there is growth in the data but that a forecasting model assuming stationarity has been used.

Suppose, for example, that the Aromco data given in Section 19.2 are expected to show an average sales outcome of 141. We can monitor the actual outcomes to see if they deviate significantly from 141. Using an α of 0.2, we would ascribe significant divergence from our expectations if the tracking signal exceeded 0.58. Table 19.2 shows the result. Again we allow the method to settle down for the first few points by constraining the tracking signal S_t to be 0.2.

Table 19.2   Trigg's tracking signal for Aromco data

Period	Data y_t	Forecast	Error e_t	E_t	M_t	S_t
1	135.00					0.20
2	140.00	141.00	−1.00	−0.20	0.20	0.20
3	160.00	141.00	19.00	3.64	3.96	0.20
4	150.00	141.00	9.00	4.71	4.97	0.20
5	130.00	141.00	−11.00	1.57	6.17	0.25
6	140.00	141.00	−1.00	1.06	5.14	0.21
7	140.00	141.00	−1.00	0.64	4.31	0.15
8	145.00	141.00	4.00	1.32	4.25	0.31
9	160.00	141.40	19.00	4.85	7.20	0.67
10	155.00	141.00	14.00	6.68	8.56	0.78
11	165.00	141.00	24.00	10.15	11.65	0.87
12		141.00				

The calculations are very similar to those in the Trigg and Leach example, so we will not labour them here. The tracking signal remains within reasonable bounds until point 9, where it reaches 0.67. Thereafter it remains above the significant value of 0.58, thereby indicating that sales have risen significantly from the average value of 141.

19.4 The cusum method

The cusum monitor also checks for systematic deviations of forecasts from actual data. However, it can also be used to detect trend changes in the data, and will often be used to make an accurate estimate of the year-end sales outcome part of the way through the year.

A prior forecast for the year's sales is required: usually this will be the annual budget. The method is as follows:

1. Take the annual forecast and split it into months.
2. Deseasonalize the monthly data for the year to date. This should now be comparable with the split of the annual forecast which we assume did not include seasonal influences.
3. Subtract the budget forecast for each month from the seasonally adjusted actual data. This gives a set of values which we can call Δ.
4. Form the cumulative sum (cusum) of the Δs.
5. Plot the cusum.
6. Identify trend changes. These should be very clear from the cusum analysis.
7. Project the cusum to the year's end from the last trend change to give a forecast revision for the year.

Suppose, for example, that we have six months of sales volume data, and a forecast (budget) for the year of 1200 tonnes. This is equivalent to a seasonally adjusted forecast of 100 tonnes per month. Seasonal influences are at their highest in March and follow the pattern of Table 19.3. The column marked 'Volume (SA)' is the result of operation 2 above. Step 3 gives the column labelled Δ, and step 4 gives the cusum column.

Figure 19.2 shows the cusum plot for this example. It can easily be seen that there is a trend change after March. On the basis of the first three months' sales we would estimate a shortfall of 80 tonnes on budget by extending the cusum line to the right-hand side of

Table 19.3 Cusum calculations

Month	Sales volume	Seasonal factor	Volume (SA)	Budget (SA)	Δ	Cusum
Jan.	93	100	93	100	−7	−7
Feb.	101	110	92	100	−8	−15
Mar.	109	120	91	100	−9	−24
Apr.	107	110	97	100	−3	−27
May	109	110	99	100	−1	−28
Jun.	102	100	102	100	+2	−26

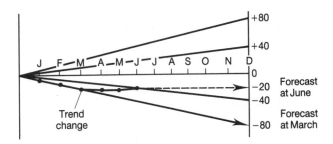

Figure 19.2   Cusum plot

the chart. However, the cusum trend from April onwards has levelled out, and by projecting this line we arrive at an updated forecast for the year's end of about 20 tonnes below budget. Experience of this technique has shown that it spots trend changes much more quickly than by looking at the raw data, and therefore allows us to amend our forecasts much more quickly.

It is worth noting that all the methods used in this chapter originated in the 1960s. Despite much research since then, these methods retain their pre-eminence.

Seasonal adjustment

20.1 Methods of seasonal adjustment

Most business and government time series are in need of seasonal adjustment. For example, industrial production shows a fall in the summer holiday period and at Christmas, and this pattern is reflected in many business series. Other seasonal influences can also be identified. For example, in the UK sales of antifreeze show two marked peaks: one in June and the other in September. The latter is due to stocking up ahead of the cold winter months, whereas the former reflects purchases by car manufacturers ahead of the new registration models available from August. (UK car sales show a pronounced upturn in August as the following year's number plates become available.)

Seasonal adjustment smoothes the trend of the data and makes one month directly comparable with another. There are many methods of seasonal adjustment available. Whichever one is used, it is important that seasonal adjustment is seen as a method of cleaning data prior to forecasting or monitoring, and not as a method of forecasting in itself.

20.1.1 Decomposition

A time series can be broken down into elements representing the trend T, cyclical movements C, seasonal variation S, and an irregular or error term E. If y represents the data, then we can describe an additive model as

$$y = T + C + S + E$$

and a multiplicative model as

$$y = TCSE$$

For example, if the third-quarter sales volume is typically 100 tonnes lower than the average quarter then we are dealing with an additive model, whereas if the third-quarter sales are usually 90 per cent of an average quarter then we have a multiplicative model. If growth is a fairly strong feature of the product history, then a multiplicative model is normally more appropriate.

Seasonal adjustment involves estimating the trend/cycle (that is, the T and C terms in aggregate) and ascribing the remaining variation (averaged over the years) as the seasonal effect. Aggregating trend and cycle in seasonal adjustment is reasonable, since the aim is to highlight seasonal influences. It is less useful when used in a forecasting context. There are three types of seasonal adjustment method:

1. Estimate trend and cycle. Estimate seasonal variation.
2. Estimate these simultaneously.
3. Estimate trend and cycle. Estimate seasonal variation. Re-estimate trend and cycle. Re-estimate seasonal variation (removal of the first estimate of seasonality may alter the trend-and-cycle estimate).

20.1.2 Methods

Simple moving average

A four- or 12-point moving average of the data y is constructed (depending on whether the data are quarterly or monthly). This moving average is itself subjected to a two-point moving average to centre the final result. Both of the moving averages have equal weights. The final moving average represents the trend/cycle and is divided into (subtracted from) the data for the multiplicative (additive) model to obtain estimates of the seasonal factors. These are then averaged by month.

This is a type 1 estimator (see Section 20.1.1) with its origin in the early 1900s. Although it can deal with both additive and multiplicative models, the moving averages used are not the most efficient in a statistical sense, and the first and last 6 months of data are effectively lost in the estimation process. No account is taken of distortions due to outliers (caused by such phenomena as strikes), and no allowance is made for the possible presence of moving seasonality (the tendency of the seasonal factor for one particular month to change gradually over the years). It is, however, a good, simple method which was used extensively in the pre-computer age.

Dummy variables

Use 12 dummy variables S_i ($i=1, \ldots, 12$) with $S_i = 1$ for data from month i, and $S_i = 0$ otherwise. Regress y on an assumed trend/cycle (for instance, a straight line $a + bt$) and $S_1 \ldots S_{11}$ which are the additive seasonal factors:

$$y = a + bt + c_1S_1 + c_2S_2 + \ldots + c_{11}S_{11}$$

Note that we cannot use all 12 S_is as regressors as $\Sigma_{i=1}^{12} S_i = 1$ and a regression equation cannot therefore be estimated. This is a type 2 estimator. Extension to the multiplicative case is more difficult. The method does not deal with extreme values or moving seasonality, and the trend/cycle term is not of the moving average form.

Holt–Winters

Holt and Winters (Winters 1960) use exponential smoothing to estimate trend/cycle and seasonal factors concurrently. This is an extension of Holt's (1957) forecasting method, allowing for non-stationarity and seasonality in the data. As such it is angled towards forecasting rather than estimating historical seasonals with maximum accuracy (for example, it does not estimate seasonal factors by using *centred* moving averages). It is a type 2 estimator of seasonal factors, and can deal with both additive and multiplicative models, but not with outliers.

Other methods

There are many other methods, most of which aim to deseasonalize data as part of a forecasting exercise. The following are some examples:

- Box–Jenkins: This (type 2) forecasting technique is a complicated representation of the data by means of lagged autoregressive (AR) and moving average (MA) variables. It can deal with seasonality by using lags of 12 months on both AR and MA factors, but this is a relatively inefficient method of describing past seasonality, and lessens the parsimony required of a good Box–Jenkins equation.
- Bayesian: As with Box–Jenkins, this is (again a type 2) adaptation of what is essentially a forecasting tool, not a way of providing optimal seasonal estimates.

20.2 The X-11 technique: history

The simple moving average technique was used during the first half of the twentieth century. It allowed stable seasonality to be estimated using a computationally simple procedure. Stable seasonality was adequate for most data subjected to seasonal analysis (mainly government economic data), given that all calculations had to be performed by hand.

From the 1950s the advent of electronic computers allowed more complex calculations to be performed quickly, and there was a greater need to extend seasonal analysis to business data. This was in general 'noisier' and subject to extreme values and moving seasonality as the business world evolved. It became clear that an iterative (Type 3) technique would be needed to model these factors in a stable fashion. The family history of the new method (the X-11 variant of the Census Method II seasonal adjustment routine) is as follows:

1920 National Bureau of Economic Research (NBER) developed the ratio to moving average method

1954 Bureau of Census computerized this

1955 MA method replaced by Census Method II

1960 First experimental version of Census II available to the public (X-3)

1961 X-9: standard program. X-10: for more variable series (included a moving average of variable length)

1965 X-11: replaced both X-9 and X-10 and became the standard program. Used by governments around the world.

1982 Kenny and Durbin (1982) suggested an amendment to X-11 which was taken up by the UK Central Statistical Office (CSO), and is now used on all UK government statistics

Note that during the course of development, Census II became available in both monthly and quarterly forms.

20.3 Overview of X-11

The following is a summary of the X-11 procedure. More detail is given in the ensuing sections.

1. Input at least 3 years' data, starting in any month.
2. Adjust data for trading-day variations and extreme values.
3. Make preliminary estimates of seasonal factors and seasonally adjusted series.
4. Refine estimates from stage 3. Estimate trend/cycle and irregular components and final seasonal factors.
5. Produce summary statistics and graphs.

The options available are as follows:

1. additive or multiplicative seasonality;
2. sigma limits for identifying extreme values (to allow for strikes and other market distortions);
3. specification of moving averages to be used to estimate the trend/cycle and seasonality;
4. whether or not to perform a trading-day regression, and if so the option to input weights for each day;
5. the length of the output.

The following tests are employed:

1. test for stable and moving seasonality;
2. test for significant trading-day variation;
3. graduated treatment of extremes — clearly extreme values are rejected, but semi-extreme values are given a reduced weight.

20.4 X-11 features

20.4.1 Trading-day regression

Sales can be affected by the number of Mondays, Tuesdays, ... in the month. The available options are:

1. To specify these weights in advance (for example, 1, 1, 1, 1, 1, 0, 0 would imply uniform sales on weekdays and no sales at weekends).
2. To allow X-11 to calculate the weights:
     (i) regressing irregular components on the number of times each day occurs;
     (ii) testing for significance using an F-test;

(iii) adjusting data by calculating monthly factors for each month based on the trading-day regression, and dividing these factors into the data.
3. To ignore the trading-day effect.

In addition, there are three possible levels of integration of trading-day effects into the final results.

20.4.2 Moving averages

The standard ratio-to-moving average technique requires a 12×2 or a 4×2 point MA. X-11 uses many moving averages:

1. 12×2 point MA (initial estimate of monthly trend/cycle);
2. 13 point Henderson MA (second estimate of trend/cycle after initial seasonal adjustment);
3. selection of 9, 13 or 23 point Henderson MA as described below;
4. 3×3 and 3×5 MAs to smooth seasonal factors by month.

The Henderson moving averages are sophisticated MAs designed to track trends in a statistically optimal fashion. They replace the less sophisticated Spencer 15 and 21 term MAs used in an earlier version of Census II. End effects are allowed for: an estimate of the trend is made throughout the range of the data (although, of course, the trend estimate at the two extremes of the data set is less robust than elsewhere). Clearly, it is sensible to use the lowest-order MA which will satisfactorily smooth the data, because this will lose the minimum amount of information from the original data. The Henderson MA chosen in X-11 depends on the variability in the data, measured as the ratio of the variability of the irregular components to the variability of the trend/cycle, as follows: if the ratio lies between 0 and 1, then the 9-point MA is chosen; for a ratio between 1 and 3.5, the 13 point MA is selected; and if the ratio exceeds 3.5, then the 23 point MA is used.

20.4.3 Extreme values

Each value is tested to see if it is an outlier. The procedure for this is as follows:

1. Calculate the estimated residual standard deviation (σ) for a 5-year period (for example, 1983−7 for data in 1985).
2. Assign zero weight to data more than 2.5σ beyond trend/cycle. Assign full weight (1) to data less than 1.5σ beyond trend/cycle. Assign weight between 0 and 1 to data between 1.5σ and 2.5σ from trend/cycle.

The values 1.5 and 2.5 are under user control.

Iterations

1. Trend/cycle estimation: An iterative method is used: σ is calculated; extremes are

removed; σ is recalculated. Values outside the 1.5σ limit are modified; the trend/cycle, the seasonals and the irregular components are re-estimated; extremes are re-estimated; the series is modified again; final trend/cycle and seasonals are estimated.
2.   Trading-day regression: Calculate the trading-day σ; remove extreme beyond 2.5σ; recalculate trading-day effects.

20.4.4 Tests

1.   Stable seasonality:

   F-ratio $=$ Between-months variance/Residual variance

2.   Moving seasonality. Analysis of variance is carried out on the highest possible number of complete years. Total sum of squares (SS) is divided into SS_{years}, SS_{months}, and $SS_{residual}$, and SS_{years} is used to construct the relevant F-test. Note that the existence of *moving* seasonality may be consistent with a non-significant result on *stable* seasonality. If there is a suspected break in seasonality within the length of the data, split the series into two and reanalyze.
3.   Trading-day variation. An F-ratio is tested for significant trading-day variation. If the user inputs his/her own factors the test is for the adequacy of the prior adjustments.

20.5   CSO version of X-11

As X-11 was used more and more on business series, a problem became apparent. Turning points in the trend/cycle of relatively 'noisy' series were only spotted some time after the event (typically 3 months later). This restricted its use as a short-term monitoring device since rapid identification of turning points is a prime property of a good business monitoring procedure. The reason for the delay before identifying turning points was the tendency of the program to reject recent points as outliers after a trend change and/or to make substantial changes to the seasonal factors (see Figure 20.1). Effectively, the nature of long moving averages is to understeer at turning points, and this results in heavy revisions both to the trend/cycle and to seasonal factors after the turning point is validated.

This problem was tackled by adding a short-term nonlinear forecasting routine to generate extra points to the right of the data. X-11 was then used to analyze the augmented series.

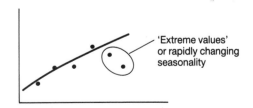

Figure 20.1 Turning point not accepted by X-11

Dagum (1979) showed that adding 12 points by an automatic Box—Jenkins routine and analyzing the augmented series gave much greater stability. This method was dubbed X-11—ARIMA. Kenny and Durbin (1982) extended this analysis to various short-term forecasting methods and used data from UK government statistics. They found that the use of any of Box—Jenkins, Holt—Winters and stepwise autoregression (a technique not described in this book) gave much greater stability to seasonal estimation on 23 UK monthly series for the period 1963—76. On average Box—Jenkins or stepwise autoregression gave the best results, although for noisy series ($MCD > 4$, where MCD stands for 'months for cyclical dominance') such as industrial data, Holt—Winters seemed to be best. The general conclusion was that, whichever forecasting method was used, a significant improvement in X-11's sensitivity seemed to result. Stepwise autoregression was seen as the best compromise in terms of simplicity, stability of the current seasonally adjusted point and stability of year-ahead seasonal factor projections. The CSO subsequently modified the X-11 routine (now dubbed X-11—CSO) for use on all relevant government statistics. However, almost any simple nonlinear forecasting device would probably be better than nothing.

It is important to realize that this improvement does not change the nature of the X-11 routine: it remains an estimator of seasonal factors and is not a forecasting device. However, the trend/cycle and seasonal factors will settle down more quickly using the CSO revision. Typically an ICI division's sales volume will correctly model a cyclical peak or trough 2 months after the event, compared with 3 months afterwards using the standard X-11 routine.

20.6 Practical points in the use of X-11

1. X-11 is used to estimate seasonal factors in past data. As a by-product a trend/cycle curve is calculated, again for past data. A tentative projection of seasonal factors for 1 year ahead is produced by a mechanical formula. No attempt should be made to project the trend/cycle beyond the data length. X-11 is *not* a forecasting device: it is legitimate to say 'a peak was passed 6 months ago' but not 'a downward trend is now in place and at the current rate will result in sales of 120 kt in 6 months' time'.

2. X-11 is a useful tool for monitoring past performance. It cleans the data and enables the user to assess the validity of short-term forecasts. For example, if the trend/cycle is pointing down and there is no evidence of extreme values in the immediate past, then a short-term forecast of a rising sales trend would need to include a reason as to why the sales trend will change direction.

3. X-11 is not perfect. It is possible for the final seasonally adjusted series to retain an element of seasonality. If this is suspected, the final seasonally adjusted series should be resubmitted to X-11 to check whether all seasonal factors for this series are 1. The advice of a statistician is required, however, as the Slutsky—Yule effect may become a problem (Kendall 1973).

4. Multiplicative adjustment is almost invariably the best option for industrial time series.

5. Consider the option of trading-day regression carefully before using it. It is an option

to use by exception only. Trading-day effects will largely be incorporated in seasonal influences: for example, February has fewer days and will therefore have a depressed seasonal factor, all other things being equal. A test on plastics sales volume some years ago showed that the effect of an extra day in the month was only to increase sales pro rata by a quarter of the expected amount — that is, sales are often linked to months and not days of the week. If, however, it is suspected that since deliveries are 'always' on a Tuesday there must be a trading-day effect, then it is worth checking out. It is important to prepare to be surprised, however!

6. The minimum data length allowed by the program is 3 years. This is realistic for stable economic series such as unemployment, but an absolute minimum of 5 years' data has been found to be necessary for most industrial data.

7. An X-11 run should be performed every month. Despite the CSO improvement, it is not unknown for seasonal estimates to change radically from month to month.

8. It is important to remember that sales volume is not the only type of data likely to involve seasonal influences. For example, unit gross margin for a group of products or a division may well be seasonal due to product mix effects.

9. X-11 should be explored. For example, it is worth omitting the early years of a data set to investigate any changes in apparent seasonality. The sigma limits are worth changing if some data points are being rejected as extremes when it is suspected that they are not. Obviously a default set of options is needed to process the bulk of the series under analysis, but the most important series probably merit some extra attention.

10. The default options seem to work very well in practice. In particular, strange results can be obtained by making apparently minor modifications to the sigma limits, and extreme care should be taken in interpreting apparently highly significant trading-day regressions. The advice of a statistician is useful in these circumstances.

11. A copy of the PC package for performing X-11 is available at low cost from the CSO.

Durbin−Watson Test ($\alpha = 0.05$)

n	$k = 1$ d_{L}	d_{U}	$k = 2$ d_{L}	d_{U}	$k = 3$ d_{L}	d_{U}	$k = 4$ d_{L}	d_{U}	$k = 5$ d_{L}	d_{U}
15	1.08	1.36	0.95	1.54	0.82	1.75	0.69	1.97	0.56	2.21
16	1.10	1.37	0.98	1.54	0.86	1.73	0.74	1.93	0.62	2.15
17	1.13	1.38	1.02	1.54	0.90	1.71	0.78	1.90	0.67	2.10
18	1.16	1.39	1.05	1.53	0.93	1.69	0.82	1.87	0.71	2.06
19	1.18	1.40	1.08	1.53	0.97	1.68	0.86	1.85	0.75	2.02
20	1.20	1.41	1.10	1.54	1.00	1.68	0.90	1.83	0.79	1.99
21	1.22	1.42	1.13	1.54	1.03	1.67	0.93	1.81	0.83	1.96
22	1.24	1.43	1.15	1.54	1.05	1.66	0.96	1.80	0.86	1.94
23	1.26	1.44	1.17	1.54	1.08	1.66	0.99	1.79	0.90	1.92
24	1.27	1.45	1.19	1.55	1.10	1.66	1.01	1.78	0.93	1.90
25	1.29	1.45	1.21	1.55	1.12	1.66	1.04	1.77	0.95	1.89
26	1.30	1.46	1.22	1.55	1.14	1.65	1.06	1.76	0.98	1.88
27	1.32	1.47	1.24	1.56	1.16	1.65	1.08	1.76	1.01	1.86
28	1.33	1.48	1.26	1.56	1.18	1.65	1.10	1.75	1.03	1.85
29	1.34	1.48	1.27	1.56	1.20	1.65	1.12	1.74	1.05	1.84
30	1.35	1.49	1.28	1.57	1.21	1.65	1.14	1.74	1.07	1.83
31	1.36	1.50	1.30	1.57	1.23	1.65	1.16	1.74	1.09	1.83
32	1.37	1.50	1.31	1.57	1.24	1.65	1.18	1.73	1.11	1.82
33	1.38	1.51	1.32	1.58	1.26	1.65	1.19	1.73	1.13	1.81
34	1.39	1.51	1.33	1.58	1.27	1.65	1.21	1.73	1.15	1.81
35	1.40	1.52	1.34	1.58	1.28	1.65	1.22	1.73	1.16	1.80
36	1.41	1.52	1.35	1.59	1.29	1.65	1.24	1.73	1.18	1.80
37	1.42	1.53	1.36	1.59	1.31	1.66	1.25	1.72	1.19	1.80
38	1.43	1.54	1.37	1.59	1.32	1.66	1.26	1.72	1.21	1.79
39	1.43	1.54	1.38	1.60	1.33	1.66	1.27	1.72	1.22	1.79
40	1.44	1.54	1.39	1.60	1.34	1.66	1.29	1.72	1.23	1.79
45	1.48	1.57	1.43	1.62	1.38	1.67	1.34	1.72	1.29	1.78
50	1.50	1.59	1.46	1.63	1.42	1.67	1.38	1.72	1.34	1.77
55	1.53	1.60	1.49	1.64	1.45	1.68	1.41	1.72	1.38	1.77
60	1.55	1.62	1.51	1.65	1.48	1.69	1.44	1.73	1.41	1.77
65	1.57	1.63	1.54	1.66	1.50	1.70	1.47	1.73	1.44	1.77
70	1.58	1.64	1.55	1.67	1.52	1.70	1.49	1.74	1.46	1.77
75	1.60	1.65	1.57	1.68	1.54	1.71	1.51	1.74	1.49	1.77
80	1.61	1.66	1.59	1.69	1.56	1.72	1.53	1.74	1.51	1.77
85	1.62	1.67	1.60	1.70	1.57	1.72	1.55	1.75	1.52	1.77
90	1.63	1.68	1.61	1.70	1.59	1.73	1.57	1.75	1.54	1.78
95	1.64	1.69	1.62	1.71	1.60	1.73	1.58	1.75	1.56	1.78
100	1.65	1.69	1.63	1.72	1.61	1.74	1.59	1.76	1.57	1.78

Source: From J. Durbin and G.S. Watson (1951), Testing for serial correlation in least squares regression, II, *Biometrika* 38: 159−78. Used by permission of the *Biometrika* trustees.

References

Abell, D.F. and Hammond, J.S. (1979) *Strategic Market Planning*, Prentice Hall.

Armstrong, J.S. (1978) *Long-range Forecasting: From crystal ball to computer*, Wiley.

Box, G. and Jenkins, G. (1976) *Time Series Analysis: Forecasting and control*, Holden-Day.

Chisnall, P.M. (1986) *Marketing Research*, McGraw-Hill.

Dagum, E.B. (1979) *The X-11*—ARIMA Seasonal Adjustment Method, Statistics Canada, Catalogue no. 12-564E.

Draper, N.R. and Smith, H. (1981) *Applied Regression Analysis*, 2nd edn, Wiley.

Fourt, L. and Woodlock, J. (1960) 'Early prediction of market success for new grocery products', *Journal of Marketing*, October, pp. 31—8.

Holt, C.C. (1957) *Forecasting Seasonal and Trends by Exponentially Weighted Moving Averages*, Memorandum no. 52, Office of Naval Research.

Johnson, G. and Scholes, K. (1988) *Exploring Corporate Strategy*, Prentice Hall.

Kendall, M.G. (1973) *Time Series*, Griffin.

Kenny, P.B. and Durbin, J. (1982) 'Local trend estimation and seasonal adjustment of economic and social time series', *JRSS*(A), vol. 145, pp. 1—41.

Kohler, E.L. (1970) *A Dictionary for Accountants*, 4th edn, Prentice Hall.

Makridakis, S. (1986) 'The art and science of forecasting', *International Journal of Forecasting*, vol. 2, p. 17.

Makridakis, S., Anderson, A., Carbone, R., Fildeo, R., Hibon, M., Lewardowski, R., Newton, J., Parzer, E. and Winkler, R. (1982) 'The accuracy of extrapolation (time series) methods: results of a forecasting competition', *Journal of Forecasting*, vol. 1, pp. 111—53.

Mensch, G. (1979) *Stalemate in Technology*, Ballinger.

O'Donovan, T.M. (1983) *Short Term Forecasting: An introduction to the Box—Jenkins approach*, Wiley.

Rogers, E.M. (1962) *Diffusion of Innovations*, Free Press.

Schumpeter, J.A. (1939) *Business Cycles*, McGraw-Hill.

Thomas, G. and DaCosta, J. (1979) 'A sample survey of corporate operations research', *Interfaces*, vol. 9, no. 4, pp. 102—11.

van Duijn, J.J. (1983) *The Long Wave in Economic Life*, Allen & Unwin.

Winters, P.R. (1960) 'Forecasting sales by exponentially weighted moving averages', *Management Science*, vol. 6, pp. 324—42.

Further reading

Bass, F.M. (1969) 'A new product growth model for consumer durables', *Management Science*, January, pp. 215–27.

Bureau of the Census (1967) *The X-11 Variant of the Census Method II Seasonal Adjustment Program*, Technical Paper no. 15, Bureau of the Census, US Department of Commerce.

Firth, M. (1977) *Forecasting Methods in Business and Management*, Edward Arnold.

Fleming, M. and Nellis, J. (1982) 'A new housing crisis?', *Lloyds Bank Review*, no. 144, pp. 38–53.

Forrester, J.W. (1976) 'Business structure, economic cycles and national policy', *Cycles*, no. 2, pp. 29–46.

Freeman, C. (1983) *Long Waves in the World Economy*, Butterworth.

Gardner, E.S. and Dannenbring, D.G. (1980) 'Forecasting with exponential smoothing: some guidelines for model selection', *Decision Sciences*, vol. 11, pp. 370–83.

Hanke, J.E. and Reitsch, A.G. (1989) *Business Forecasting* (3rd edn), Allyn and Bacon.

Harrison, P.J. (1967) 'Exponential smoothing and short-term sales forecasting', *Management Science*, vol. 13, pp. 821–42.

Harrison, P.J. and Davies, O.L. (1964) 'The use of cumulative sum (cusum) techniques for the control of routine forecasts of product demand', *Operations Research*, vol. 12, pp. 325–33.

ICI (1964) *Cumulative Sum Techniques*, ICI Monograph no. 3, Oliver & Boyd.

Kalish, S. (1985) 'A new product adoption model with price, advertising and uncertainty', *Management Science*, vol. 31, pp. 1569–85.

Ledolter, J. and Abraham, B. (1984) 'Some comments on the initialisation of exponential smoothing', *Journal of Forecasting*, vol. 3, pp. 79–84.

Lewis, J.P. (1965) *Building Cycles and Britain's Growth*, Macmillan.

Lilien, G.L. and Kotler, P. (1983) *Marketing Decision Making: A model building approach*, Harper & Row.

Mass, N.J. (1978) 'Economic fluctuations: a framework for analysis and policy design', *IEEE Transactions*, vol. SMC-8, no. 6, pp. 437–49.

Newberry, F.D. (1952) *Business Forecasting: Principles and practice*, McGraw-Hill.

Saunders, J.A., Sharp, J.A. and Witt, S.F. (1987) *Practical Business Forecasting*, Gower.

Shearer, P.R. (1982–3) 'Trade cycles and business planning', *Plastics Today*, Winter/Spring, pp. 18–21.

Trigg, D.W. (1964) 'Monitoring a forecasting system', *Operational Research Quarterly*, vol. 15, pp. 271–4.

Wheelwright, S.C. and Makridakis, S. (1985) *Forecasting Methods for Management* (4th edn), Wiley.

Wind, Y., Mahajan, V. and Cardozo, R. (1981) *New Product Forecasting*, Lexington Books.

Index

adopters, 152
advertising, 152
autocorrelation, 52−5
autocorrelation function, 129
autoregression, 25
autoregressive models, 52−62

Bass model, 151−3
Bayesian forecasts, 173
bias, 134
bimodal cycle, 84
Boston Consulting Group, 155
bottom-up forecasts, 5
Box−Jenkins forecasts, 29, 59−61, 173, 177
Brown's method, 44−7

capital equipment, 94, 104
concave diffusion models, 146−50
construction cycle, 94−102, 139
consumer demand, 69
consumer durables, 67, 94
counter-cyclical, 73−5
cross-correlation function, 129, 136, 156
CSO version of X-11, 176
Cusum method, 169−70
cyclical data, 13, 23, 157

debt, 105
decision making, 6
decomposition, 63, 171
Delphi technique, 11
demographic, 98
deterministic forecasts, 7
discontinuous data, 10
dummy variables, 130, 172
Durbin−Watson test, 25, 121

eclectic forecasts, 7
econometric models, 68
end-use analysis, 143
epidemiological diffusion models, 151−3
experience curves, 155
exponential smoothing, 41−4
extreme values, 11, 175

feedback loop, 105
forecasting accuracy, 16
Forrester, J.W., 67, 94, 104

Gompertz, 90
graphing, 9−14
gross margin, 154, 161

herring-bone effect, 141
heteroscedasticity, 119
hierarchical analysis, 5
Holt's method, 47−9
Holt-Winters' method, 50, 172, 177
homoscedasticity, 119
housing, 94, 96−100
housing stock, 97

ICI, 36, 98, 102, 106, 107, 116, 177
indices, 37
inflation, 72
innovation, 106
interest rates, 70, 72

Kondratieff, 103

lagged responses, 135
lagged variables, 129
leading indicators, 76−8

life cycle, 85–7, 145
logistic, 90
long wave, 103–10

Makridakis, S., 8
margins, 154–9
mean absolute deviation (MAD), 17
mean absolute percentage error (MAPE), 17
mean squared error (MSE), 17
Mensch, G., 106
modified exponential, 90
monitoring, 6, 165–70
moving average, 18, 41, 172, 175
moving seasonality, 12, 174
multicollinearity, 123
multiple cycles, 92
multivariate forecasts, 7

naive forecast, 17, 40
NEDO, 102
new product models, 141–53
non-demographic demand, 100
nonlinearity, 137
non-repurchasable products, 145

oil crisis, 96, 107
oil prices, 65, 113–16
OPEC, 115
out-of-sample fitting, 31–4
overfitting, 128

partial autocorrelation coefficient, 55
partial F statistic, 127
peak-to-peak forecasting, 78–83
pipeline effect, 68, 138
planning model, 160-4
planning process, 1, 6
price hysteresis, 158
prices, 37, 154–9
price-volume lag, 156
product maturity, 86, 134
product parallels, 144

random walk, 57
rebasing, 37
regression, 125–31
regression assumptions, 119–24
replacement-purchase products, 145
repurchasable products, 145
residual analysis, 22–34
revision error, 38, 133
ridge regression, 125–7

sawtooth cycle, 84
scenarios, 1, 112
Schumpeter, J.A., 108
seasonality, 12, 171–8
sensitivity analysis, 29–31
serial correlation, 120–3
share prices, 56, 72
shocks, 113
simulation, 65–8
Slutsky-Yule effect, 177
STATGRAPHICS, 28, 56, 58
stationary data, 9
stepwise autoregression, 177
stepwise regression, 127–8
stocks, 66, 68, 70
substitution, 138
S-curve diffusion models, 150

top-down forecasts, 5
trade, 37
trade cycle, 63–85, 137
trade cycle clock, 72
trading-day regression, 174
transformations, 14–16, 120
trend curve analysis, 88–92
Trigg's tracking signal, 167–9
Trigg–Leach forecast, 165–7

unemployment, 72, 98, 107, 109
univariate forecasts, 7

van Duijn, J.J., 107

X-11, 11, 63, 81, 173–8